For my husband, Howard.

FABULOUS FAKES

A Passion for Vintage Costume Jewelry

CAROLE TANENBAUM

Photography by Puzant Apkarian

AN ARTISAN / MADISON PRESS BOOK

Published by Artisan
A Division of Workman Publishing, Inc.
708 Broadway
New York, New York 10003-9555
www.artisanbooks.com

Library of Congress Cataloging-in-Publication Data

Tanenbaum, Carole
Fabulous fakes : a passion for vintage costume jewelry / Carole Tanenbaum.
p. cm.
ISBN-13: 978-1-57965-290-0
ISBN-10: 1-57965-292-1
1. Costume Jewelry. I. Title.

NK4890.C67T36 2006
688'.2'075—dc22

2005051307

Printed in China

10 9 8 7 6 5 4 3 2 1

Contents

INTRODUCTION   6

Chapter One
VICTORIAN ERA & ART NOUVEAU (1837–1914)   8
Romantic, Sentimental, Bold

Chapter Two
ART DECO & PREWAR (1920–1935)   36
Luxe, Exotic, Graphic

Chapter Three
POST-DEPRESSION & THE WAR YEARS (1936–1949)   62
Restrained, Feminine, Elegant

Chapter Four
THE FIFTIES (1950–1959)   102
Optimistic, Opulent, Glamorous

Chapter Five
THE SIXTIES & SEVENTIES (1960–1979)   160
Artisanal, Permissive, Global

Chapter Six
THE EIGHTIES & NINETIES (1980–1999)   188
Garish, Minimal, Severe

Chapter Seven
INTO THE TWENTY-FIRST CENTURY (2000–present)   204
A Return to Fabulous

Collecting Vintage Costume Jewelry   212
Glossary   214
Acknowledgments and Credits   218
Index   220

Introduction

I have a confession to make: I am an incurable collector and always have been. I come by it honestly—my parents were avid art collectors. I can remember my father sitting for hours with new acquisitions, studying their forms and researching to find out all he could about them. It was our family routine to gather and talk about each newfound treasure. These discussions were the basis for my approach to collecting. I am forever grateful to my parents for their inspiring curatorial scholarship and enthusiasm.

Although my parents' wisdom influenced my aesthetic education, I have developed a singular point of view in my own collecting, whether it is paintings, textiles, photography or vintage costume jewelry. In the early seventies, my husband, Howard, and I went to see a collection of vintage costume jewelry in London, England. I was immediately drawn to the colors, scale and designs—a kaleidoscope of gems. I was hooked and my passion for fabulous fakes hasn't abated. Today, there are more than 3,500 pieces in my private collection and more than 8,000 pieces in the retail Carole Tanenbaum Vintage Collection.

My collection is developed from a personal perspective. I don't have examples of jewels by every fine costume jeweler, just the ones whose designs interest me. My favorite decades for twentieth-century costume jewelry are the fifties and sixties. As a result, I have many more pieces from mid-century than I do from other periods. *Fabulous Fakes* reflects the proportions and preferences of my collection. It's a treasure chest of my favorites, rather than a general reference on costume jewelry.

The three qualities that I look for in selecting pieces for my collection are originality, fine workmanship and good condition.

Originality in design is paramount. I am drawn to jewels that are unique, quirky and recognizable. I prefer the original concepts created by designers such as Sandor, Schreiner and Schiaparelli to the great gem-revival designers such as Boucher.

Workmanship is a second consideration when I'm assessing a possible acquisition. Quality and unusual construction set apart the highly collectible pieces, including those of Sherman or Haskell, from merely "pretty" jewelry. Unusual or beautiful settings interest me. In fact, I often find the back of a piece as fascinating as the front.

Finally, condition is important to me. I try to buy pieces in the best, closest to original, condition possible. I don't believe in extensive restoration. I would rather pass on pieces that have been heavily restored. I never buy anything that has been reconstructed. Many dealers replace stones to make an item look "fresh." However, I value the patina, even the irregularity, that comes with age, since it gives the jewelry integrity and history.

In *Fabulous Fakes*, I will share with you the history of costume jewelry through the decades. But mainly I will share my passion. I hope that when you study the collection you will look at vintage costume jewelry not as a substitute for precious or gemstone jewelry but as a craft with great integrity and beauty unto itself. Costume jewelry charms, perplexes and continues to intrigue me. My hope is that this book will make a collector of you.

Carole Tanenbaum

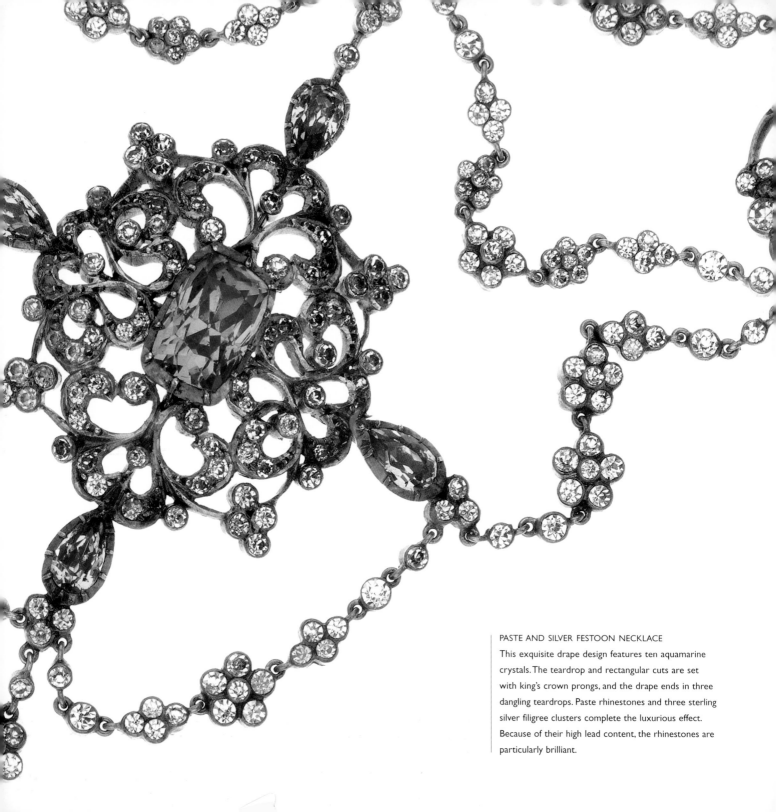

PASTE AND SILVER FESTOON NECKLACE

This exquisite drape design features ten aquamarine crystals. The teardrop and rectangular cuts are set with king's crown prongs, and the drape ends in three dangling teardrops. Paste rhinestones and three sterling silver filigree clusters complete the luxurious effect. Because of their high lead content, the rhinestones are particularly brilliant.

Victorian Era & Art Nouveau

(1837–1914)

ROMANTIC, SENTIMENTAL, BOLD

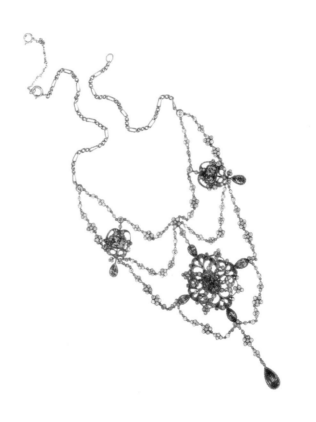

MONKEY BROOCHES
Charles Darwin's *On the Origin of Species by Means of Natural Selection*, published in 1859, inspired interest in insects, monkeys and other animals. These sparkling monkeys *(above and opposite)*, remarkably human in form, are of paste and sterling silver, with small crystal eyes.

On June 28, 1838, nineteen-year-old Alexandrina Victoria was crowned Queen of England at Westminster Abbey, one year after her accession to the throne. For the next sixty-three years, Queen Victoria's romantic and sentimental nature and her great love for Prince Albert—not to mention her love of personal adornment—would strongly influence the motifs, materials and designs of costume jewelry. Many new jewelry styles were created during this period, along with design revivals influenced by the Renaissance and Egyptian eras.

The increasing demand for fashionable jewelry and clothing during the nineteenth century was fueled in large measure by a growing middle class in Europe. Thanks to the Industrial Revolution, designers could now create bold and regal pieces using the latest technological innovations. And the quality of the craftsmanship often rivaled that of fine jewelry. Jacquin of Paris, for example, developed a method for making fake pearls by coating hollow balls of blown glass with a mixture of varnish and ground fish scales. Georges Stras, also of Paris, made long-lasting paste jewelry with a compound of glass mixed with white lead oxide and potash. In the Czech Republic, machine cutting expanded the production and availability of low-cost large stones that were often colored with foil backing to increase their hue and brilliance. And in Birmingham, England, cut steel, which had originally been used in the making of swords and shoe buckles, was now crafted into settings for marcasite (poor man's diamonds).

The pageantry and romance of Queen Victoria and Prince Albert's wedding in 1840 captured the public's imagination and sparked an immediate interest in romantic and sentimental jewelry. Mizpah pins, also known as love brooches, were soon being worn by all economic classes.

Made of silver and engraved with the names or initials of loved ones, these charming pins often featured motifs that conveyed symbolic messages: ivy leaves, for friendship; bluebells, for constancy; ferns, for fascination; hearts, for charity; and tail-eating serpents, for eternal love. (The serpent motif was a particular favorite of Queen Victoria, whose betrothal ring was shaped like a snake.) Lovebirds, hearts, cupids, arrows, hands, ribbons, bows, crosses and anchors were also popular.

Queen Victoria
and the Prince Consort,
Prince Albert

Hair jewelry—including brooches, chokers and bracelets—came back into fashion at this time as well. Made of tightly woven hair pieces that were glued and mounted as assemblages in pins, hairwork was originally worn in the eighteenth century as memento mori or as mourning jewelry. By the mid-nineteenth century, however, the hair of living loved ones was being fashioned into keepsakes. Miniature paintings or portraits were placed on the pins, often with ground hair as the coloring agent. Queen Victoria, in fact, received a brooch on her sixteenth birthday made of her mother's hair. She was so enchanted with the concept that after her betrothal to Prince Albert she was never without a lock of his hair. Although some find the idea of hair jewelry distasteful today, its popularity during the Victorian era in England, America and France was undeniable. If we view hair art as romantic tokens and understand the intricacy of the craftsmanship, we can appreciate the beauty of the pieces.

TORTOISESHELL PUTTI
(ANGEL) BRACELETS
These bracelets are
unusual both for their
intricate carving and for
their excellent condition.
Because tortoiseshell is
brittle, most pieces from
the Victorian era are
chipped or cracked and
few survived the period.

In 1852, Queen Victoria purchased the Balmoral Estate in Scotland—immediately launching a craze for all things Scottish, including the country's distinctive agate and silver jewelry. Made of three different varieties of agate, the striking jewelry required the work of many skilled artisans, including silversmiths, engravers, stonecutters and jewelers. Other dramatic stones, such as citrines, amethysts, smoky-orange cairngorms, carnelians, bloodstones and jasper, were also incorporated in Scottish designs—as was malachite, a vivid green mineral imported from Siberia by way of Germany. Popular motifs were inspired by traditional Celtic plaids, eternal knots, clan symbols, crests and shields. Silver pins in the shape of dirks, or small knives, were often worn on kilts. Another popular Scottish design, the Luckenbooth, featured two entwined hearts with a crown above. This token of love was also meant to protect against evil spirits.

By 1870, there were more than one thousand artisans working in Edinburgh in the jewelry trade to satisfy the droves of tourists who visited the region each year. Also added to the Scottish repertoire were nontraditional forms such as pendants, earrings and bracelets. Very few of these pieces were signed, but collectors can recognize Scottish vintage jewelry by the "C" clasps on pins and by the unique construction and designs of the period.

In 1861, Prince Albert succumbed to typhoid—plunging Queen Victoria and her subjects into a long period of mourning. By royal decree, only jet could be worn at court. Jet is a coal-like, carbonized black substance formed by heat, pressure and chemical reaction on ancient driftwood. Originally used during the Bronze Age for small personal items, it was fashioned into prayer rosaries and crosses in medieval England. The finest jet was mined at Whitby, on the Yorkshire coast of England, and by the mid-1800s there were more than 1,400 people employed there in crafting jet for adornment.

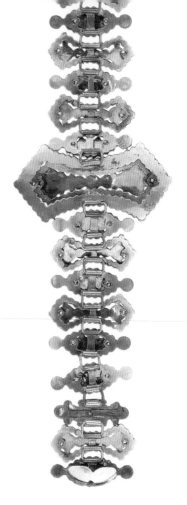

GARNET BRACELET
With its square wire connectors and small brass knobs that fasten the layers, the construction of the front (not shown) and back of this piece is typical of Bohemian garnet jewelry.

FRENCH JET COLLAR
Economical and sturdy,
French jet was ideal for
intricate constructions
such as this. The square-
cut glass stones are
domed, with flat backs set
in black-painted metal.

The lightweight, easy-to-carve substance was perfect for large, dramatic earrings or for enormous brooches with moving parts. It was frequently faceted to reflect light and was also paired with shell cameos, cut-steel studs, silver buckles and aluminum. French jet, a black glass backed with lead, was not as fragile as natural jet, making it suitable for more intricate and delicate earrings and brooches in the shape of flowers, stars and hearts—all connected with invisible wire.

While Queen Victoria mourned her beloved Albert until her own death in 1901, the nation eventually grew weary of black attire and its attendant mourning jewelry. By the 1880s, the Whitby-based jet industry was in serious decline, affected as well by the many inexpensive substitutes for jet that continued to flood the market.

Yet despite the lower cost of mass-produced goods, including jewelry, not everyone embraced factory-made items. Victorian women of means frequently rejected the shoddily made jewelry on offer, preferring to purchase from artists and craftsmen. The Arts and Crafts movement of the 1870s was a reaction to inferior machine-made products. Its leaders, William Morris and John Ruskin, promoted handmade designs based on floral and primitive forms. In the early 1900s, the French-based Art Nouveau movement elaborated on the themes of nature and fertility, turning to a highly stylized nature for its inspiration. Pieces from this period include melancholic botanical pins, dragonflies and *femme-fleur*, which featured women's faces with flowing hair arising from flowers and leaves. Much of this jewelry was made with "humble" materials such as horn, glass and enamel. Ironically, the demand for these designs led to mass-produced pieces—and the movement eventually dissipated. Still, it anticipated a new era as it embraced both nature and technological change in the expression of its art.

As the Victorian era drew to a close at the beginning of the twentieth century, women's lives—as well as their clothing—became marginally emancipated. Suffragettes demanded the right to vote (and to wear bloomers) and the yards of undergarments, crinolines, corsets and bustles that women were compelled to wear gradually gave way to a new fashion for crisply tailored suits and the sporty charm of the Gibson girl.

DRAGONFLY BROOCH
Plique-à-jour, a method of enameling that gave pieces greater life and shimmer, was used by both costume and fine jewelers of the Victorian era. The centerpiece of this gold wire brooch is a stunning oval Crackled Ice sapphire cabochon. The dragonfly's eyes are prong-set pearls.

BOHEMIAN SPLENDOR IN GLASS

Rococo designs with semiprecious stones on filigree
backgrounds characterize Bohemian-style jewelry.

NECKLACE WITH PENDANT

With its irregularly cut semiprecious stones, bezel-
set in elaborate cups, this extravagantly designed
pendant can also be worn separately as a brooch.
The swan, with its single free-form pearl wing, sits
on a filigree garland of flowers. The delicate
necklace is of gold filigree openwork.

NECKLACES AND BRACELET
(Far left) The court-like
necklace with pendant has
a carved green-glass cameo,
chiseled in relief and bezel-
set in a braided border.
(Left) Mother-of-pearl
accents on openwork silver
filigree give this colorful
enameled necklace delicacy
and grace. *(Above)* This gold-
filled bracelet features an
intricate floral enamel
pattern surrounding an
unusual, highly faceted,
prong-set crystal.

HAIRWORK AND PORTRAIT BROOCHES

The fashion for hair jewelry began in the eighteenth century
and continued through the Victorian era.

HAIRWORK BROOCHES AND BRACELET

(Top) Swivel brooches, such as these, were commonly worn to commemorate
betrothals, weddings or the death of a loved one. They feature hairwork on one
side and hand-painted portraits on porcelain or ivory on the other—often set in
frames of twisted, gold-filled metal. *(Above)* Individual strands of human hair were
woven together, then braided, to form the band of the bracelet. Note the key
design surrounding the portrait.

PORTRAIT AND PANSY BROOCHES

Hand-painted portraits, like the ones below, were often given as gifts.
(Bottom, right) This swivel brooch bears the inscription "E. W. Welsh. From her
fond brother Horace, 1875." *(Bottom, left)* The pansy brooch has particularly
beautiful iridescent milk glass and amethyst glass set in a frame of ruffled ribbon
and four domed, engraved cartouches.

PASTE AND COURT JEWELRY

Museum-quality paste brooches such as these from the
Victorian era are very difficult to find. When Napoleon
became Emperor of France in 1804, he revived the
fashion for ostentatious displays of wealth.

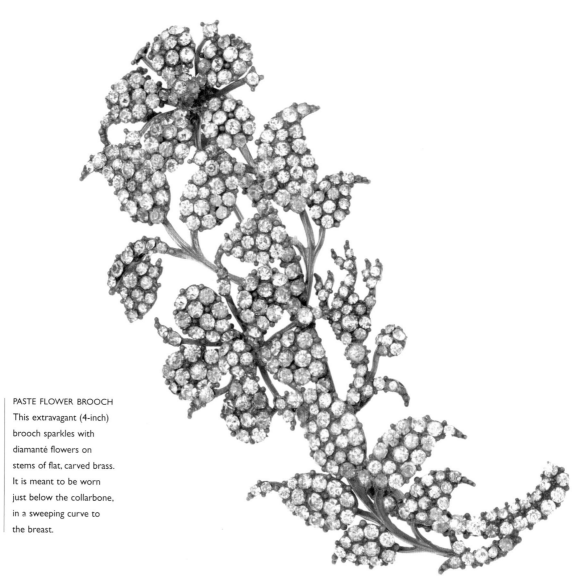

PASTE FLOWER BROOCH
This extravagant (4-inch)
brooch sparkles with
diamanté flowers on
stems of flat, carved brass.
It is meant to be worn
just below the collarbone,
in a sweeping curve to
the breast.

BROOCHES AND BRACELETS

(Below, far left and left) These two brooches are of clear paste in open-structured settings. The peacock's tail articulates a curve of variously sized stones with a feathered accent of small peridot chaton-cut stones. The bow brooch has an unusual openwork ruffled border. *(Below, right and far right)* The four-hinged bracelet has five separate sections filled with clear stones. The delicate floral motif of the bracelet to the far right is supported by alternating silver links. *(Bottom)* The large oval navette-cut sapphire crystals of this bracelet are typical of the Austro-Hungarian style.

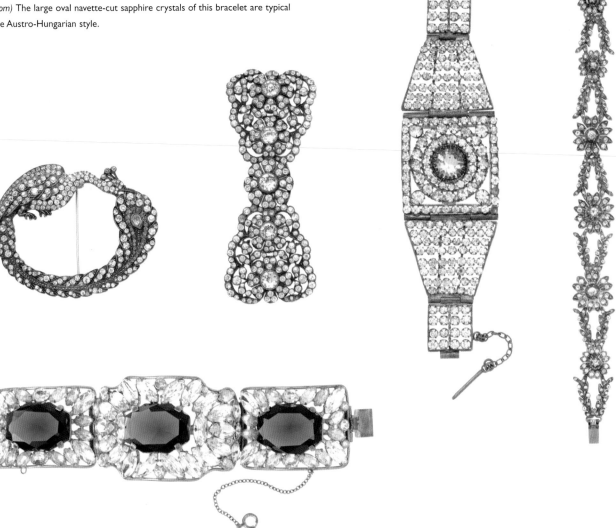

BOG OAK AND JET MOURNING JEWELRY

Bog oak, preserved for thousands of years in peat bogs,
was ideal for carving into jewelry and other decorative objects.

BRACELETS AND BROOCHES
(Above and right) These delicate wreath-shaped
bog oak brooches are rare finds. *(Top, right)* These
bracelets are of vulcanite, a sturdy option for
designers creating mourning jewelry. *(Top, left)* The
portrait bracelet, of Whitby jet, features a young
girl's image painted on porcelain.

FRENCH JET AND CUT STEEL

Cut steel consists of tiny nails, individually faceted and polished, set on studs mounted into brass plate. Since the process was so laborious, few pieces were produced. This necklace is collectible because all of its original extensions are intact.

INSPIRED BY NATURE

The Victorian fascination with nature resulted in realistic depictions of the "sublime" in art and fashion.

BRASS PARURE AND FUR CLIP
This set, featuring coral glass beads dangling from brass leaves, exemplifies the Art Nouveau style. A double snake chain completes the necklace of concave brass leaves and free-floating coral grapes. Two butterflies flit among the leaves of the fur clip *(top)*.

INSECT NECKLACE WITH PENDANT

The Egyptian Revival style is apparent in this very
long (longer than opera length) necklace with huge,
faceted, amber-colored bezel-set stones. The scarab,
or beetle, motif was especially popular with
Victorians.

BIRMINGHAM SILVER

The Industrial Revolution brought
steam power and efficient machinery
to the domestic production of silver
in the United Kingdom. Birmingham,
England, was known as the "toyshop of
the world" because its silver was factory-
produced and internationally marketed.

BRACELET AND LOCKET

(Above) Engraved with an intricate leaf motif, this
buckle bracelet features three-dimensional silver balls
as accents. *(Right)* Images of birds in flight on the locket
make a fashionable reference to the asymmetrical
aesthetic of Japanese design. The gold-overlay pendant
hangs from a necklace of looped, heavily engraved links
connected by large rings.

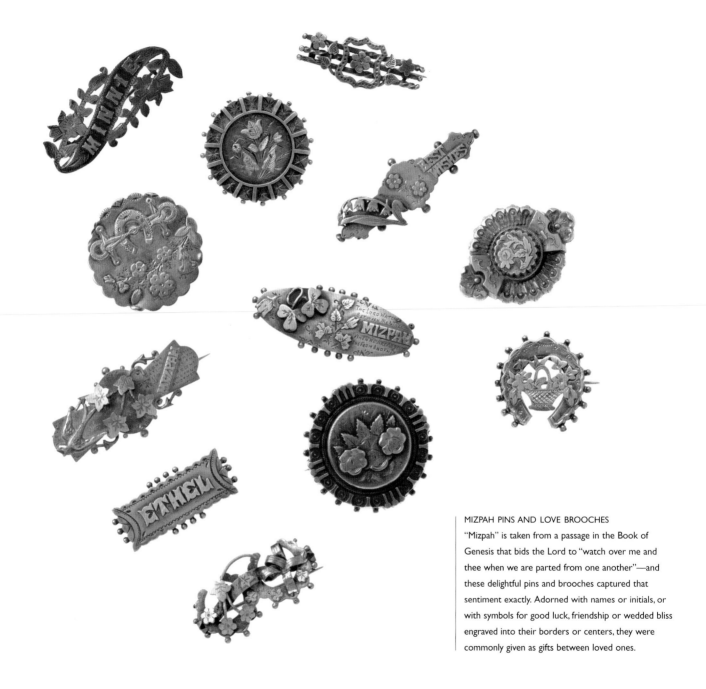

MIZPAH PINS AND LOVE BROOCHES

"Mizpah" is taken from a passage in the Book of
Genesis that bids the Lord to "watch over me and
thee when we are parted from one another"—and
these delightful pins and brooches captured that
sentiment exactly. Adorned with names or initials, or
with symbols for good luck, friendship or wedded bliss
engraved into their borders or centers, they were
commonly given as gifts between loved ones.

EGYPTIAN REVIVAL

An interest in all things Egyptian was expressed through decor and adornment.

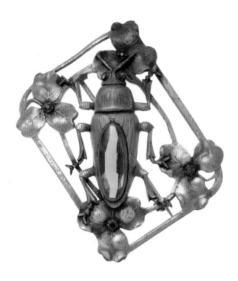

EGYPTIAN REVIVAL NECKLACE WITH PENDANT
(Left) A pharaoh's portrait in relief is the focal point of this necklace. The amber-colored glass is set in concave brass filigree and accented with vivid yellow and blue beads. *(Above)* The sash pin exemplifies the Egyptian Revival style, with its beetle's belly of amber crystal surrounded by four smaller chaton-cut crystals.

SASH PINS

Sash pins were worn in a variety of ways—on the hip,
in the center of a blouse or on hats.

SASH PINS

(Top, left) Delicate floral filigree is surrounded by a brass frame with a key design.
Stones are emerald-cut peridot. *(Top, right)* With its oval, faceted, amber-colored
stones, prong-set and flanked by fashionable silver pansies, this pin is pure drama.
(Bottom, right) Wise owls are set atop hammered brass with a central bezel-set
amethyst crystal. *(Bottom, left)* Simulated coral and double layers of lacy filigree
celebrate the Art Nouveau style.

THE DRAMA OF FRENCH JET

Since French jet is actually glass, it is durable and easy to carve. It was the material of choice for many artisans working on delicate and intricate designs.

INSECT BROOCHES

These fanciful brooches are constructed with small metal fixtures. The jet is flat-backed and faceted, glued on black-painted metal backings. Because these pieces were soft-soldered, few examples survive today.

COLLAR NECKLACE
Each faceted jet stone
is set on a separate metal
disk in this elaborate
necklace. The closure is
an ingenious invisible
double hook at the back.

SCOTTISH MALACHITE AND GRANITE

Immensely popular with the Victorians, Scottish jewelry was an interesting blend of the ornate and the austere carved out of natural stones in alluring hues of green, gray and pink.

GRANITE AND AGATE BROOCHES
The sensual carved brooches convey softness and luxury, in marked contrast to the stark, bold lines of the silver-and-agate anchor and the cairngorm-topped dirk. (Above) Swirls of granite, agate and bloodstone are woven into this intricate brooch, with its extended pinback.

MALACHITE AND GRANITE TREASURES

A sterling silver engraved heart closure is sentimental in design *(far left),* while the impressively heavy malachite bracelet *(center left)* is more formal, with its hand-engraved silver border. *(Bottom)* These malachite brooches offer a range of styles, with engraved silver and cushion-cut malachite, and a buckle-strap brooch signifying the Order of the Garter. The brooches in granite are detailed studies with sterling silver embellishments.

SCOTTISH PLAID JEWELRY

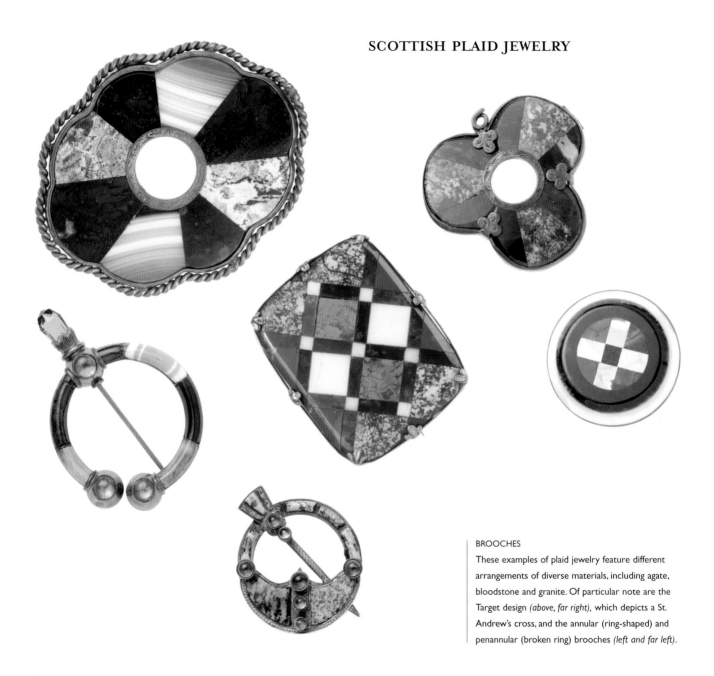

BROOCHES

These examples of plaid jewelry feature different arrangements of diverse materials, including agate, bloodstone and granite. Of particular note are the Target design *(above, far right),* which depicts a St. Andrew's cross, and the annular (ring-shaped) and penannular (broken ring) brooches *(left and far left).*

AGATE PADLOCK AND BUCKLE BRACELETS
Agate bracelets were available to the Victorians in
dozens of attractive designs and materials, including
(from top) bloodstone and goldstone; agate and silver;
cairngorm, with a checkerboard pattern; cushion-cut
agate; and agate and silver. Note the shield- and
heart-shaped padlock closures.

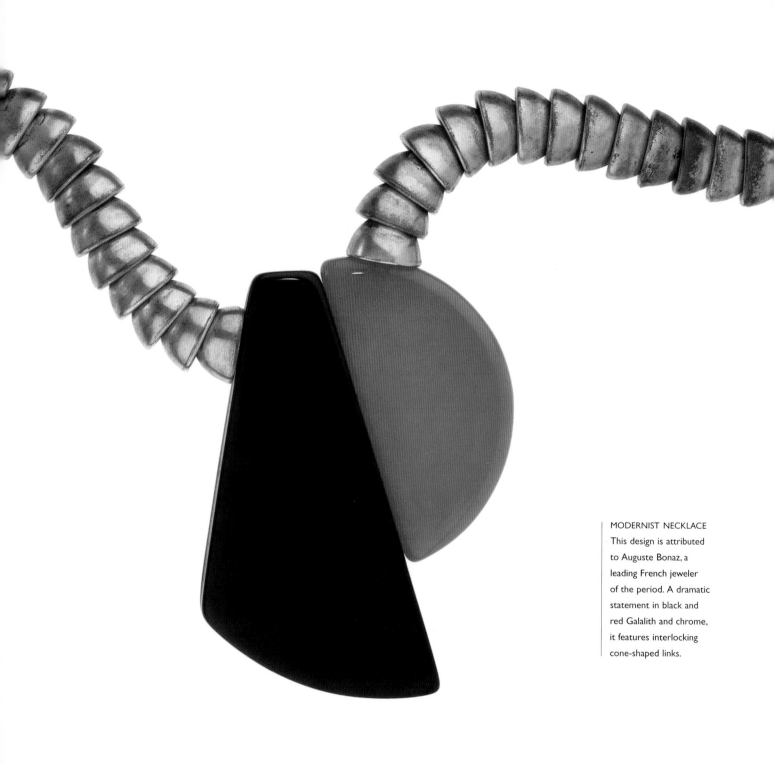

MODERNIST NECKLACE
This design is attributed
to Auguste Bonaz, a
leading French jeweler
of the period. A dramatic
statement in black and
red Galalith and chrome,
it features interlocking
cone-shaped links.

Art Deco & Prewar

(1920–1935)

LUXE, EXOTIC, GRAPHIC

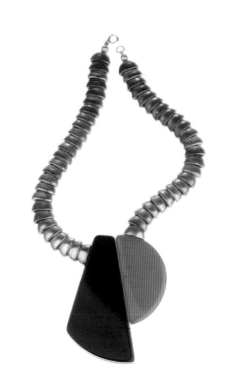

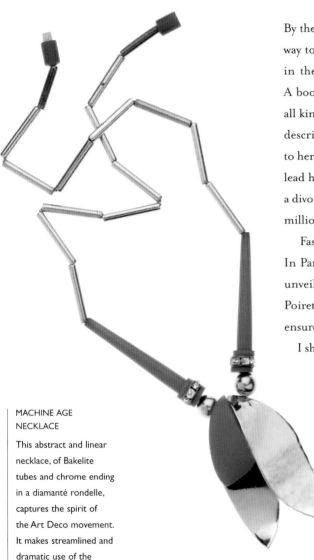

MACHINE AGE NECKLACE

This abstract and linear necklace, of Bakelite tubes and chrome ending in a diamanté rondelle, captures the spirit of the Art Deco movement. It makes streamlined and dramatic use of the popular leaf motif.

By the early 1920s, the virtuous, demure, tightly corseted female had given way to a new style of woman—emboldened by her newly won right to vote in the United States, and freer in her dress and her public behavior. A booming postwar economy, which created an appetite for indulgence of all kinds, fueled the fires of emancipation. *Vogue* magazine, in a 1923 issue, described this new woman: "The vamp. A very special brand. You propose to her by telephone and marry her by wireless. You do not make a home and lead her in, but mix a cocktail and take her out. She will probably demand a divorce on the grounds of incompatibility of dance steps. Only suitable for millionaires."

Fashion designers eagerly interpreted "the look" of the new woman. In Paris, Madame Vionnet, Jean Patou, Jeanne Lanvin and Charles Worth unveiled a new, bias-cut silhouette that moved freely with the body. Paul Poiret, on the other hand, proposed some restraint with his hobble skirt, to ensure that women were not *too* unencumbered. "Yes, I freed the bust, but I shackled the legs," he explained. The majority of designers, however, placed no restrictions on their liberating creations. Gone were the bustles, crinolines and corsets—replaced by slinky dresses, short skirts and tube-like chemises that demanded entirely bolder and more luxurious accessories. Short haircuts, worn to achieve the popular *garçonne* look, required long pendant earrings to feminize the appearance. And the sinuous shape of flapper dresses begged for multiple beads and bangles.

Enraptured by the explosion of new design talent at the *Exposition Internationale des Arts Décoratifs et Industriels Modernes* in 1925, the leaders of the Art Deco movement swept away the emotive and figurative oeuvre of Art Nouveau and replaced it with a love of linear, abstract and streamlined shapes that echoed the new Machine Age. For the first time, costume jewelry was influenced by socioeconomic changes in the form of new art movements—Dadaism, Surrealism, Cubism, Futurism, Bauhaus—as well as by changes in social mores and by industrial innovations in manufacturing, travel and communications.

INITIAL BROOCH
A charming house-shaped brooch, with initials cut through the sterling silver backing, is embellished with marcasite and channel-set emerald-colored baguettes.

By the 1920s, women had definitely broken free of Victorian constraints. Note the saucy hand on hip and the crossed, stockinged legs.

GERMAN BROOCH AND NECKLACE
(Above) This beautiful brooch consists of meticulous enamelwork and marcasite stones in a sterling setting. *(Below)* A German bracelet, attributed to Theodor Fahrner, features large, semiprecious chalcedony stones set in an elaborate gold metal frame.

Gérard Sandoz, a leading artist jeweler of the era and one of the organizers of the 1925 *Exposition*, eloquently captured the vision of this new intellectual and artistic movement: "Let us open our eyes wide: to cinema, to distorted images of things seen at high speed, the beauty of machine parts skillfully made; to the understated magnificence of sleek surfaces, of luxury liners, of contemporary painting; to aviation, syncopated music, the power-assisted brake, the cocktail shaker, the telephone, steel and nickel, lights and shades, mechanics and geometry. We are all this. We are simply living our time. This is the modern base of everything which we create and which we will create in the future."

And what a time it was! In smoky jazz clubs, sipping a *cocktail de la mode* (Dubonnet and gin, "half and half and shaken very cold"), fashionable women sported rows of bracelets, long strands of *essence d'Orient* pearls, with Swarovski aurora borealis-like crystal *sautoirs*. They swanned about in evening scarves made of silk, monkey fur, leopard skin or satin, topped with an aigrette-festooned silk turban and diamanté à la Josephine Baker in the hit theatrical *La Revue Nègre*. It was the age of luxury, and nothing was *de trop* in the realm of jewelry. To satisfy women's passion for opulence, American

designers Trifari, Napier, Marcel Boucher and Eisenberg adapted their paste pieces from precious jewelry created by Cartier and by Van Cleef & Arpels.

Thanks to the durability and affordability of the new plastics Bakelite and celluloid, costume jewelry designers boldly experimented with shape and color as they had never done before. Soon fashionable women were boasting bracelets, brooches and necklaces in flat, geometric designs with dramatic color combinations: black and white; green, red and mustard; gold-flecked aventurine and carnelian. The artist Auguste Bonaz, for example, created striking modernist statements in contrasting shapes of Bakelite. And Theodor Fahrner, a manufacturer in Pforzheim, Germany, mass-produced inexpensive clips and pins in marcasite and silver fashioned into bows, circles, arrows, flowers and animal figures.

But the Machine Age was not the only inspiration of the period. The discovery of Tutankhamen's tomb in 1922 sparked an Egyptian revival in dress and jewelry—particularly pavé-set paste jewelry bearing images of reclining Nubian maidens, hieroglyphics, birds, cobras and other Egyptian symbols. In 1934, Claudette Colbert starred as Cleopatra, providing a much-needed escape for a society still smarting from the stock market crash of 1929. Napier, the American costume jewelry house, introduced a complete line of accessories under the name Spirit of Ancient Egypt— including brass-winged brooches decorated with beetles, scarabs and much blue-green enameling. Other popular motifs included stars, crescents, palm trees and exotic designs in enamel, jade and green glass that evoked the *Arabian Nights*.

GERMAN STERLING FLAMINGO BROOCH

Like other figurals of the period, this flamingo of pavé-set marcasite has detailed enameling and beautiful gradations of color. Its 2-inch size is larger than most contemporary figural brooches.

The fashion and jewelry of the Roaring Twenties mirrored the decade—carefree, opulent and decidedly elegant.

Tutankhamen may have sparked a fashion revival, but it was Coco Chanel and Elsa Schiaparelli who ignited a fashion and costume jewelry revolution. Chanel opened her first boutique in Paris in 1913, followed by another in the resort town of Deauville. A year later, her Maison de Couture was the shop of note in Biarritz, another posh seaside resort. Rival designer Paul Poiret, who still promoted the languid look of turbans and tight skirts, dismissed Chanel's simple and sporty wool gabardine tunics as *poverty de luxe*.

Mindful that her signature fashions would require embellishment, Chanel also launched a line of costume jewelry featuring gargantuan, obviously fake pearls; large Byzantine- and Slavic-inspired paste jewelry; and the bold designs of Madame Gripoix. For Chanel, what mattered was the ornamental value of jewelry, not the cost. Fortunately, she traveled in aristocratic circles and was able to hire members of European royalty, who were well acquainted with fine jewelry, to create her collections. Comte Etienne de Beaumont launched her paste jewelry line, and Duc Fulco di Verdura created many of her most enduring pieces—including the Maltese Cross bracelets copied by Kenneth Jay Lane in the 1960s. Chanel once said to Madame Gripoix, "All those aristocrats stuck up their noses at me but I'll have them at my feet," and, indeed, her fierce talent and her feisty temperament made her prophecy come true.

Elsa Schiaparelli launched her career in 1927 with a line of whimsical knitted sweaters boasting trompe l'oeil bowknots. While Chanel was influenced by the opulent lifestyles of her wealthy and royal lovers, Schiaparelli's inspiration, particularly for accessories, came from her collaborations with the avant-garde artists of the time, such as Salvador Dalí. In 1928, she opened Schiaparelli Pour le Sport at 4 rue de la Paix in Paris, where she sold an expanded range of items—including coats and skirts with buttons, zips, hooks and buckles that looked like jewelry.

Schiaparelli hired Jean Clément to design her signature zany buttons in the shapes of shoelaces, spinning tops, coffee beans and lollipops. Alberto Giacometti, then a member of the Surrealists, created a series of gilt metal brooches and buttons in gorgon, siren, bird and angel figures. Schiaparelli also commissioned Jean Schlumberger to design Victorian-inspired cherub pins and brooches in the shape of a hand. By the mid-thirties, Schiaparelli would create entire *bijoux fantasie* collections to coordinate with her seasonal fashion offerings.

The stock market crash of 1929 sent the era of indulgence into a tailspin. Yet the fashionable woman's love affair with jewelry showed no signs of waning. The Depression, a looming war and the imposition of a luxury tax in France all spurred the costume jewelry industry, which turned to less expensive materials such as chrome, plastic, steel and frosted glass to fashion its pieces. And as people flocked to movie houses for a few hours of escape, Hollywood costume designers and ingenues became the new arbiters of style. Both Chanel and Schiaparelli were savvy enough to jump on board.

CZECH ENAMEL BROOCH

Inspired by the Bohemian jewelry of the late nineteenth century, this jewel of a brooch is a delicate marriage of white enamel and stonework. Each gem is bezel-set and rests on a filigree backing.

MACHINE AGE TREASURES

This selection of jewelry celebrates the bold,
geometric lines of the Machine Age.

BAKELITE BROOCHES
AND BRACELETS

Each of these pieces combines
chrome or brass with Bakelite
in a dramatically different
way—from the soft lines of
the blue ruffle bracelet from
Germany *(left, center)* to the
gas-pipe chrome bracelet *(left,
bottom)*, which is rigid in form.

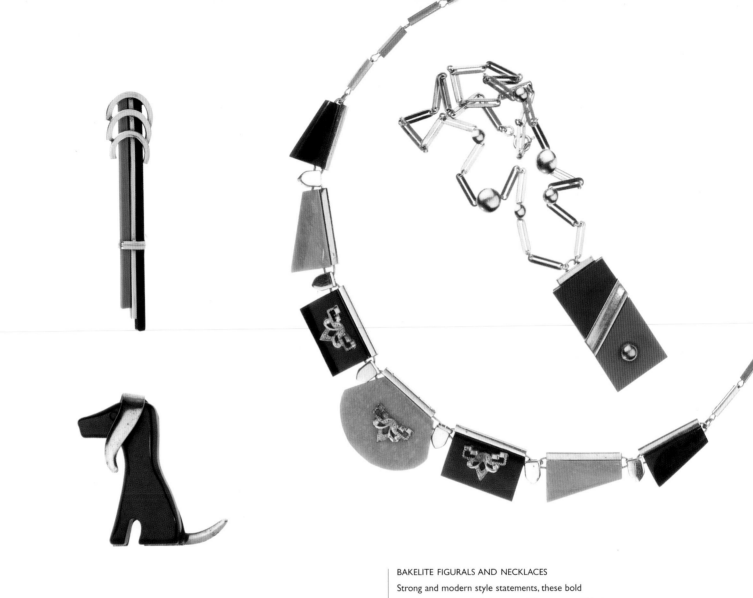

BAKELITE FIGURALS AND NECKLACES

Strong and modern style statements, these bold
designs were ahead of their time. The green-and-black
Bakelite necklace *(above)* is a beautifully feminine
design, featuring soft lines and brass accents.

Signature ELEMENTS

THEODOR FAHRNER

Theodor Fahrner began mass-producing jewelry in 1855, in Pforzheim, Germany. The designs, usually by German artists, were of high-quality sterling and marcasite, and cost more than most costume jewelry.

Prior to the mid-1920s, the company was known for its Art Nouveau, Arts and Crafts and Celtic Revival styles—in abstract designs with fanciful motifs in enamel and paste. Through the 1920s, with the advent of the Jazz Age, Fahrner introduced bold, geometric pieces.

Theodor Fahrner died in 1919. The company was taken over by Gustav Braendle, who continued production until 1979.

GERMAN STERLING, FRENCH NECKLACES

The artistry of Art Deco included intricate German sterling silver creations and the more delicate designs of French jewelers.

STERLING BRACELETS AND BROOCH
(Left) The Theodor Fahrner bracelet of glowing rock crystal, amazonite and chalcedony is signed "T.F." It was designed and manufactured in the 1920s.
(Above) This bracelet and brooch are also attributed to Fahrner, although they are unsigned. They are certainly German enamel and sterling.

FRENCH NECKLACES

(*Far left*) Note the unusual construction of this
necklace, with its mesh and knotted chain.
(*Center*) Cushion-carved frosted glass is prong-set
in sterling with an octagonal emerald crystal in its
center. The simple chain is accented with elegant pearls.
(*Above*) A beautifully carved emerald crystal is set off by
paste stones and triangular emerald crystal accents.

THE SPARKLE AND WHIMSY OF BROOCHES

Worn singly or in clusters, brooches and clips were the ultimate fashion accent.

DECO BROOCHES AND CLIPS

(Above) With its geometric formality, this dress clip makes a classic Deco style statement. *(Below)* The double-swirl diamanté brooch has a blue cabochon center and prong-set marquis stones, rhinestones and baguettes. *(Left, top)* The angular sweep of this brooch is inspired by a Cartier design. *(Left, center)* This elaborate initial pin is in sterling open scrollwork. *(Left, bottom)* A circular fur clip was de rigueur on the tail of one's fur stole.

GERMAN STERLING ENAMEL FIGURALS
German figural brooches are among the finest
and most intricate enamelwork in costume jewelry.
Generally very small in scale, these treasures have
multiple gradations of color and are beautifully
sculpted on sterling silver.

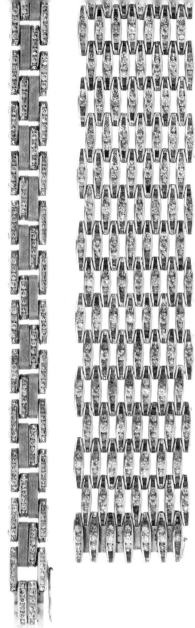

A PATENT FOR EXCELLENCE

The German patent mark DRGM (Deutsches Reichs-Gebrauchsmuster) was used from 1891 through the 1950s by many anonymous craftsmen in their Art Nouveau and Art Deco designs. Much of the DRGM jewelry is in geometric arrays of clear, crystal stones set in zinc alloys.

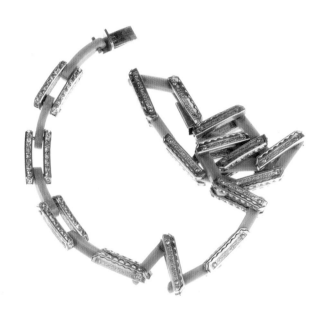

BRACELETS AND NECKLACE

Each of these bracelets is typical of the DRGM style: geometric, flexible and perfectly symmetrical. Often, the jewelry is as beautiful on the back as it is on the front. The bracelets are of the following materials: *(far left)* Bakelite and channel-set crystals; *(left)* channel-set rhinestones; *(right, back view of construction)* Bakelite and steel. *(Above)* The necklace is of alternating links of Bakelite and rhinestones. Note its flexibility.

NECKLACE, EARRINGS AND FUR CLIP

The black necklace is a typical DRGM design, with its alternating Bakelite and channel-set rhinestone links. Each link is joined so that the necklace is articulated. The earrings *(left)* and fur clip *(above),* of channel-set rhinestones, exemplify stylish simplicity.

ART DECO BRACELETS

Creations by Cartier and by Van Cleef & Arpels were often the inspiration for Art Deco bracelets. The attention to detail and craftsmanship lavished on the costume pieces rivaled that of fine jewelers. For stylish profusion, these bracelets were worn in multiples.

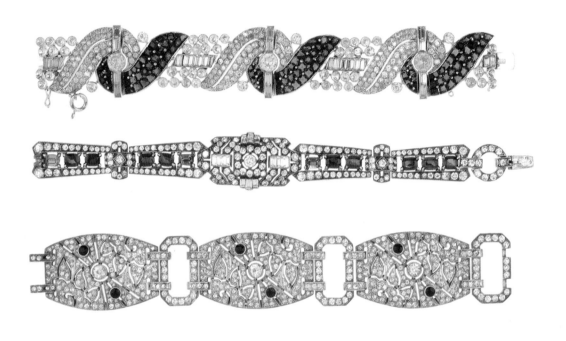

DECO DELUXE

All the bracelets above are of sterling silver with rhinestone pavé and variously colored stones. Note the regularity of the patterns and the luxurious number of crystals for maximum sparkle. *(Right)* This bracelet, with its bright coral stones and emerald crystals, has individually linked rectangles, which make it very flexible.

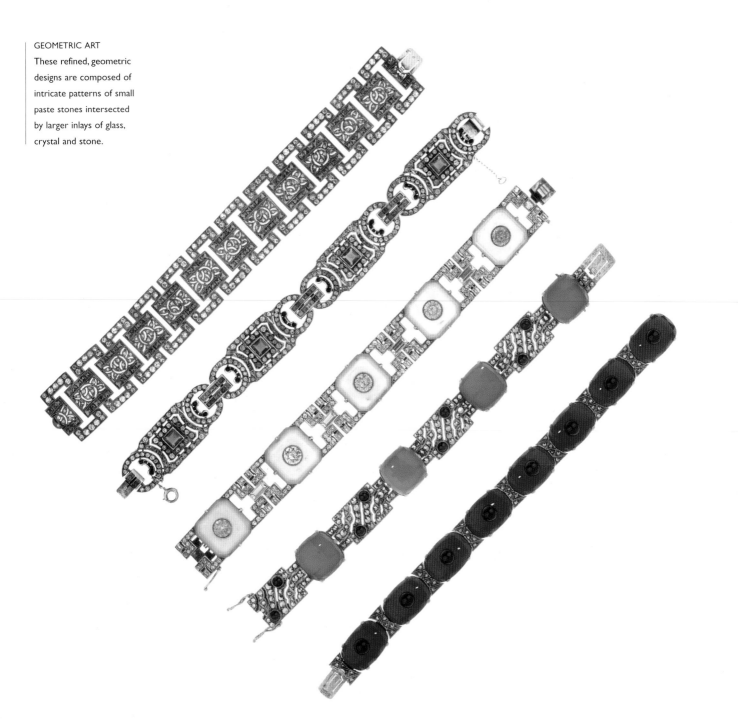

GEOMETRIC ART
These refined, geometric
designs are composed of
intricate patterns of small
paste stones intersected
by larger inlays of glass,
crystal and stone.

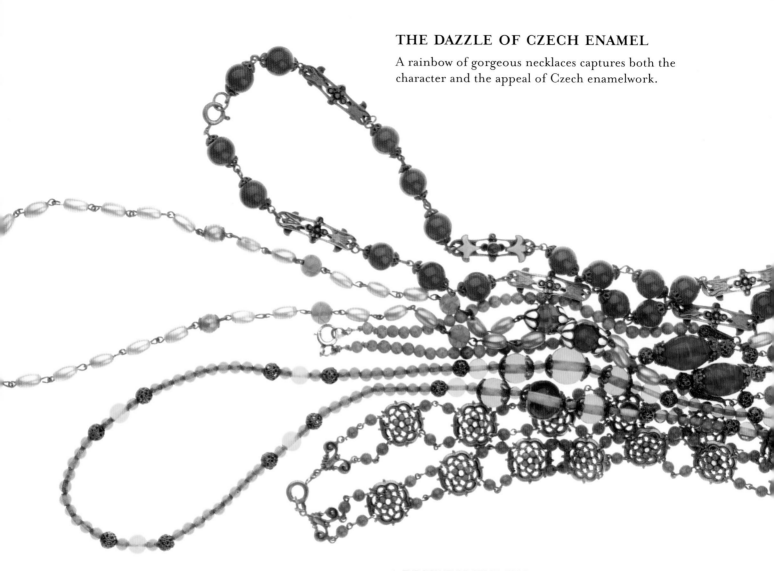

THE DAZZLE OF CZECH ENAMEL

A rainbow of gorgeous necklaces captures both the character and the appeal of Czech enamelwork.

THE SIGNATURE CZECH STYLE

All these necklaces are on elaborate filigree backings with bezel-set stones. There are examples of faceted round crystals in striking color combinations; rosette enamel and stone links; tube- and teardrop-shaped glass beads of brilliant hues; and enameled open-back dangling stones at the ends of the necklaces—a signature Czech style.

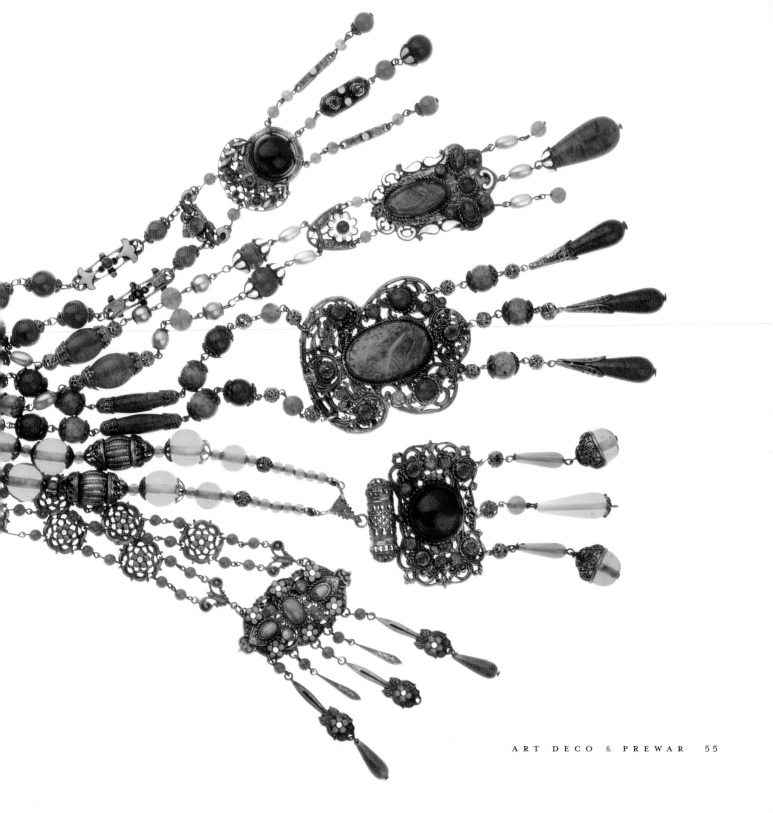

RENAISSANCE REVIVAL

Elaborate filigree, enamel and stone bracelets typify both the Renaissance Revival style and the Czech style. *(Above, left)* Rectangular filigree links and enameled green leaves make a perfect foil for green, oval bezel-set crystals. *(Above, right)* Each rectangular filigree link has different enamel leaves in its corners. *(Center)* Amber stones are surrounded by a black enamel border and connecting enamel links. *(Right)* These unusual pinched blue crystals are set off by a hexagonal enamel border. *(Far right)* Green cabochons glow against a closed filigree background and white enamel centers.

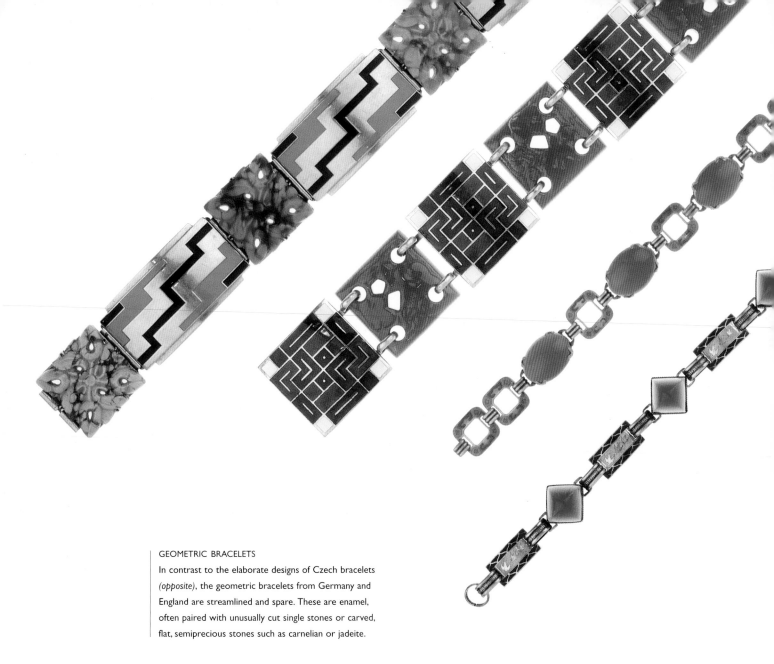

GEOMETRIC BRACELETS

In contrast to the elaborate designs of Czech bracelets
(opposite), the geometric bracelets from Germany and
England are streamlined and spare. These are enamel,
often paired with unusually cut single stones or carved,
flat, semiprecious stones such as carnelian or jadeite.

CZECH CRYSTALS AND FILIGREE

No country used colored stones as abundantly or as beautifully as Czechoslovakia did. Flower baskets and butterflies were among the most popular subjects through the 1930s.

FILIGREE BROOCHES

These filigree brooches are of particular interest because of their glorious arrays of colorful crystals. *(Left)* Although this delightful brooch is 4 inches wide, it is graceful. *(Above)* The closed basket-weave filigree makes a perfect setting for the star-shaped emerald crystal at the heart of this brooch.

CZECH FIGURALS

As these whimsical brooches prove, every color combination presented by Czech artisans seems to work. *(Bottom, left)* The 4-inch butterfly shows color at its most creative.

APPLE JUICE BAKELITE AND CELLULOID

Apple Juice is among the most sought-after of all types of Bakelite.
Celluloid presented an alternative to Bakelite for costume jewelers
who preferred its moldable convenience.

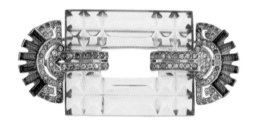

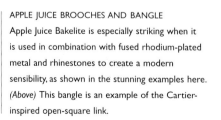

APPLE JUICE BROOCHES AND BANGLE

Apple Juice Bakelite is especially striking when it
is used in combination with fused rhodium-plated
metal and rhinestones to create a modern
sensibility, as shown in the stunning examples here.
(Above) This bangle is an example of the Cartier-
inspired open-square link.

FANTASY IN CELLULOID

This stack of beauties is a small sampling of the wonderful designs and colors found in celluloid bangles of the 1920s and 1930s. Softer than Bakelite, celluloid enabled jewelers to imbed decorative rhinestones and crystals that make the bracelet sparkle. The more intricate the design, the more collectible the piece.

BAKELITE

Bakelite, a phenolic resin that can be molded and cast into countless different shapes, was patented in 1907 by Dr. Leo Baekeland.

After its initial application in industrial designs, Bakelite was produced in beautiful colored translucents, and costume jewelers took note. Because it was versatile and affordable, it became a popular material for artisans, particularly during the cash-strapped Depression years.

In the 1940s, Bakelite patriotic jewelry appeared, mainly as keepsake brooches for the sweethearts of departing soldiers. After the war and into the early 1950s, Bakelite designs became more intricate, and matched sets began to appear on the market. It was Bakelite's heyday.

Style changes in the mid-fifties marked the decline of Bakelite's popularity, and it was now used more as an accent than as a primary medium. By the 1970s, Bakelite's moment was officially over.

Today, Bakelite jewelry is highly collectible.

HASKELL PROTOTYPE BEADED NECKLACE

In the late 1930s, Haskell introduced an innovative line of economical wooden jewelry. Among the most marvelous of the pieces is this six-strand collar of deep purple and green wooden beads, accented with flat, beaded clusters in the shape of flowers. The center of each flower is a combination of clear, fluted beads and yellow seed beads.

Post-Depression & the War Years

(1936–1949)

RESTRAINED, FEMININE, ELEGANT

RETRO DRAMA
This elegant brooch, set
in sterling vermeil with
a single emerald-cut
crystal, captures the Retro
style at its very best. The
large circle sparkles with
pavé-set clear rhinestones,
as does the point at the
base of the three chains.
The concept is modern
and dramatic.

By the mid-1930s, magazines such as *Vogue* were heralding a return to dressing up. For a younger generation, the tribulations of the Depression were all but forgotten. There was renewed excitement about adornment, abetted by the innovation of color fashion photography and the popularity of glossy magazines and catalogs. For the first time, middle-class women could feast their eyes on images of brightly colored gems, instead of only pearls, platinum and white diamonds—the workhorses of black-and-white photography. At the depth of the Depression, the average American earned $1,000 a year, and a quarter of the population was unemployed. Now, post-Depression fashion editorials proclaimed that jewelry was the way to a woman's heart:

> Husbands do not have to be told that nothing equals jewelry for restoring the lost gilt of romance in marital relations. There's something illicit about jewels, and wives adore illicit presents.
>
> It makes them feel like movie mistresses. —*Vogue*, 1934

Few Americans could pony up at Tiffany, yet many more could indulge in the costume pieces intended to look like the real thing that now flooded the market.

"Cocktail-style" was the hallmark of faux jewelry in the mid- to late-1930s: bossy, show-off pieces such as knuckle-duster rings, gilt metals and double-clips. The hard lines of Art Deco and modernism were supplanted by sensuous shapes in warm-gilded finishes, enamel and sparkling paste stones. Factories, many based in Rhode Island, produced these voluptuous designs for the mass market. Pennino, one of my favorite design firms, was the leader in this style. Its pieces were exuberant, asymmetrical floral, bow and ribbon motifs in rose pink or yellow gilt metal—with pins measuring up to 5 inches in diameter. Only the finest Austrian rhinestones in invisible settings were used, and the Italian craftsmanship was impeccable. (I prefer Pennino pieces that have fewer stones and more gold vermeil to better showcase the artistry and creativity.) Macy's department store promoted the new "gold rush" with golden jewelry from Trifari, Monet and Napier as a way to brighten up utilitarian black clothes.

The looming war in Europe effectively shut Paris out of the American fashion market and irrevocably changed American tastes. Irreverent books, such as Elizabeth Hawes's *Fashion Is Spinach*, asserted American independence from European dictates—as did Fifth Avenue department stores that created window displays touting the American Look. Hollywood stars Joan Crawford, Greta Garbo, Marlene Dietrich, Jean Harlow and Norma Shearer wore immaculate clothes by the American costume designers Gilbert Adrian and Travis Banton. They often accessorized their outfits with large Retro jewelry pieces that referenced Art Deco designs. The Golden Age of Hollywood glamour now seduced the factory worker and the shopgirl by removing fashion's elitist connotations. And women's magazines featured many famous actresses in photo spreads, reinforcing the Hollywood fashion message.

During the war, because cloth was rationed (sixty-six coupons for clothing, the same as for margarine), costume jewelry was used to boost morale. By 1945, sales of costume jewelry in the United States had tripled. Patriotic jewelry—frequently in

VOGUE BOW BROOCH
Vogue's signature designs are exemplified by its early bow brooches. This 5-inch brooch has prong-set, unfoiled crystals that appear to float inside a wire outline.

Until the mid-1940s, most advertisements for Haskell jewelry were published in *Women's Wear Daily* and local newspapers. The ads were detailed to show how the pieces should be worn.

red, white or blue Bakelite—bolstered the idea of the American Dream with images of soaring eagles, flags, trumpets, drums and slogans like "Remember Pearl Harbor." These pieces were worn to show support for the war and were often given as gifts for the sweethearts left behind. (Interestingly, red pieces proved to be slow sellers because consumers associated the color with communism.)

Jewelry factories were converted into sites for the manufacture of bullets and radio parts. With sparkling Austrian crystals in short supply, designers ingeniously used Bakelite, Lucite, wood, glass, shell and other low-cost materials to experiment with mass jewelry as they never had before. (Designers Trifari and Eisenberg also used silver during the war, but discontinued it afterward as it was costly and tarnished easily.)

Alfred Philippe at Trifari produced a range of whimsical animal figurals, called Jelly Bellies—fish, swans, birds, poodles, penguins and lizards—using large polished cabochons of Lucite that resembled rock crystal. Lucite had

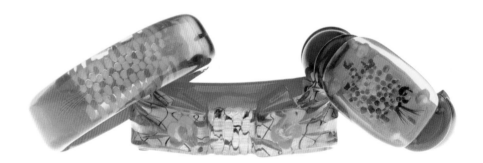

BAKELITE BANGLES
These reverse-carved Apple Juice Bakelite bangles have opaque backs and transparent fronts in painted floral motifs.

previously been used in the thirties with Bakelite or wood in a coarser fashion. When I began to collect Jelly Bellies, neither I nor the original owner of a vast collection knew their importance or their value. Today, I always carry one of them in my pocket when I'm scouting for new pieces because although there are many expensive copies today, the originals are more delicately constructed, especially in the facial features. Coro, another large American jewelry manufacturer, produced similar pieces but was sued by Trifari for copying its designs.

Trifari also produced small-scale enamel pins with the crafts-manship of *miniatura*. These pieces, including the rare monkey-man pin, show in the colored enameling astonishing detail that implies movement and naturalistic expression. They completely charm me, and I collect them the way I used to collect stamps: whenever I find one, I buy it. Many of these pieces, including the wheelbarrow and the flower carts, would have been considered "feel-good" jewelry and quickly discarded. However, some of the designs, such as the unusually colored violet and chartreuse iris pins, were probably custom pieces.

In the forties, Miriam Haskell transformed rather unglamorous mate-rials such as wood, beads and shells into poetic pieces of costume jewelry. (I was fortunate to meet Eli and Sandy Moss, who were the owners and managers of Haskell manufacturing in the 1980s, and I was able to acquire some prototype pieces from them.) Haskell used wood in pins and in elaborate rosette collars as no other designer did. The cost of producing the collar and the gorgeous crystal beaded runway necklace for mass distribution would have been prohibitive.

ENAMEL FIGURALS
Meticulously cast silver figurals by Trifari and Coro are brightly enameled, giving them the quality of fine miniatures. Many figurals, such as the rare monkey-man above, are very collectible.

Another great designer of the forties is Marcel Boucher, who worked for the firm of Mazer (which specialized in hand-set flower jewels) before launching his own business. Formerly with Cartier, Boucher created a range of abstract-looking animal figurals. His owl, bird and elephant pins in pink-gold vermeil, with a single emerald-cut stone in the center, have a spontaneous yet tailored look. Boucher's enamel pieces have an aqueous, dreamy quality to them, evoking an aura of unparalleled grace. They were probably not made for mass production.

Eisenberg is another highly collectible name in costume jewelry. Originally a dress manufacturer, the company switched production to jewelry-making when its pin accessories proved even more popular. Usually marked "Eisenberg Originals," the firm's work included beautiful and glitzy pins, many with bow motifs and hand-set large crystals, that adorned Hollywood stars.

I believe that William Hobé—who began his career by creating costumes and jewels for the Ziegfeld Follies in the twenties and later made jewels for Hollywood stars such as Bette Davis and Ava Gardner—is an underrated talent in costume jewelry. Descended from a family of Parisian gold- and silversmiths, Hobé's signature pieces—floral bouquet brooches in sterling silver or gold vermeil with fine crystals and semiprecious stones in his favorite shades of rose quartz, topaz, amethyst and blue sapphire— show great refinement. Jewelry advertisements in the 1940s and 1950s frequently used movie stars as models with taglines that referred to the opulence of the costume pieces.

Other important manufacturers during this period include Vogue, Coro, Sandor and Silson. Vogue was a small producer of high-quality handmade pieces. Its signature construction was open-back set stones that allowed light to pass through the crystal. Many pieces also featured stones set in brass cup-like surfaces. Silson was an American designer who specialized in patriotic jewelry but who also made some wonderful limited-edition, large-scale tremblant pins in crystal and vermeil. Sandor created beautiful enamel pins but also Rococo-like bracelets in the forties that are objets d'art. The quality of the design and metalwork proves him to be an artist, not simply a costume jeweler. Coro, a U.S.-based manufacturer that specialized in mass-market pieces, created the famous Duette pin of the forties. This was an ingenious design: the large brooch could be split in two for real versatility. The Coro company also produced under the labels Coro Craft (upscale line) and Vendome (couture line).

Carmel Snow, then the editor of *Harper's Bazaar*, advised her readers, "If precious stones are beyond you...the road to glitter in 1937 is paved with huge and humorous jewels." A decade later, women would be influenced by a new decree: the New Look.

On February 12, 1947, Monsieur Christian Dior showed his new spring collections, "Eight" and "Corolla," at his Avenue Montaigne atelier. It was like a luxury bomb explosion. Wasp waists, endless yards of expensive fabrics, and off-the-shoulder décolletés announced a new, haute-feminine way for women to dress after the parsimony of the war years. Dior also carefully hand-picked faux jewels to coordinate with each sumptuous ensemble. There was an immediate anti-New Look uproar in America—women who dared to wear the designs were physically attacked on the street—but top retailers embraced the trend, paving the way for the opulent, optimistic and over-the-top 1950s.

RETRO BRACELET
With strong, clean lines and a bold geometric design, this quintessential Retro bracelet features sterling vermeil and a single, large, emerald-cut crystal that is unfoiled, open-back and prong-set. Tiny pavé-set clear and red rhinestones adorn each side of the center stone.

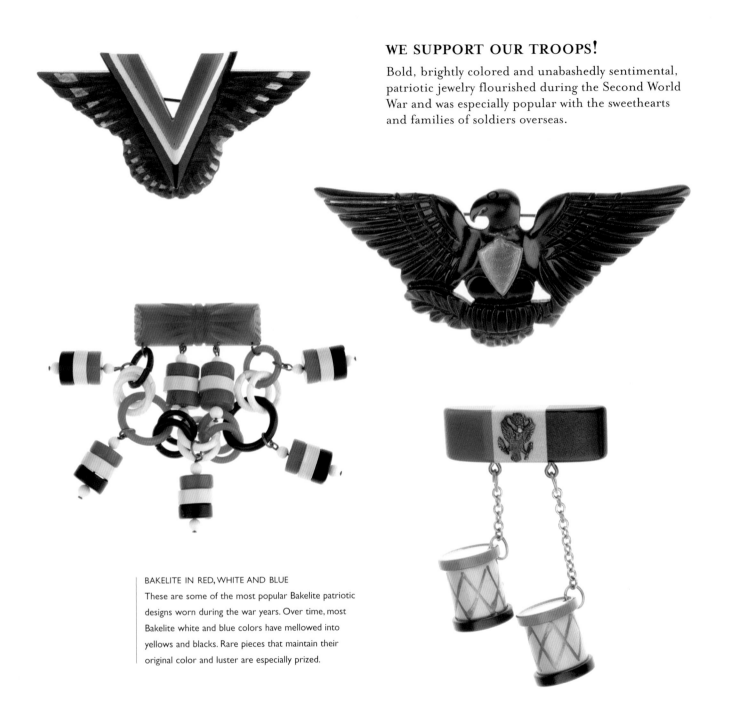

WE SUPPORT OUR TROOPS!

Bold, brightly colored and unabashedly sentimental, patriotic jewelry flourished during the Second World War and was especially popular with the sweethearts and families of soldiers overseas.

BAKELITE IN RED, WHITE AND BLUE
These are some of the most popular Bakelite patriotic designs worn during the war years. Over time, most Bakelite white and blue colors have mellowed into yellows and blacks. Rare pieces that maintain their original color and luster are especially prized.

PATRIOTIC BROOCHES

"Long May It Wave." The American flag was a natural motif in patriotic jewelry, as was the eagle. *(Above, right)* Rippling in silver with red and navy enameling, this flag is of pot metal and tiny, clear rhinestones. *(Above, center)* The rare USA map brooch is edged in black enamel, with open spaces forming the states' perimeters. *(Above, left)* This eagle is cleverly rendered in red and blue faceted baguettes. *(Top)* Large, clear rhinestones appear to float in an open gold-wire eagle frame.

JELLY BELLIES AND OTHER DELIGHTS

Some of the more unusual Jelly Belly brooches were produced by Trifari and Coro.

JELLY BELLY BROOCHES
(Right) The most collectible of Trifari's Jelly Bellies is the elephant, part of a series by Alfred Philippe. This example is rhodium-plated. The tusks, eyes and tail are enamel. *(Far right, top)* An elegantly manicured hand holds a vermeil flower with a teardrop-shaped pearl accent. *(Far right, bottom)* Balancing on one leg, this heron has rhinestone plumage and a tiny red cabochon eye.

A LITTLE BIT OF WHIMSY

These delightful figurals are Bakelite combination brooches. *(Top, left)* The graceful dog has a marbleized opaque Bakelite head with a clear Lucite backing. *(Top, right)* The carved Bakelite and Lucite lobster features hand-painted rope antennae. *(Bottom, right)* This reverse-carved fan is of fluted Lucite. *(Bottom, left)* With its carved wooden body and Lucite face, the elephant is an unusual marriage of materials.

BAKELITE MASTERPIECES

The wonderful versatility and affordability of Bakelite allowed
designers unlimited freedom in transforming the moldable
resin into delightful—and dazzling—works of art.

RARE FINDS

The Bakelite brooches here are all quite rare.

(Left) The floral brooch is possibly a French prototype
because of its soft carving and delicate construction.

(Above, left) The frog's articulated arm actually moves
to "strum" the banjo.

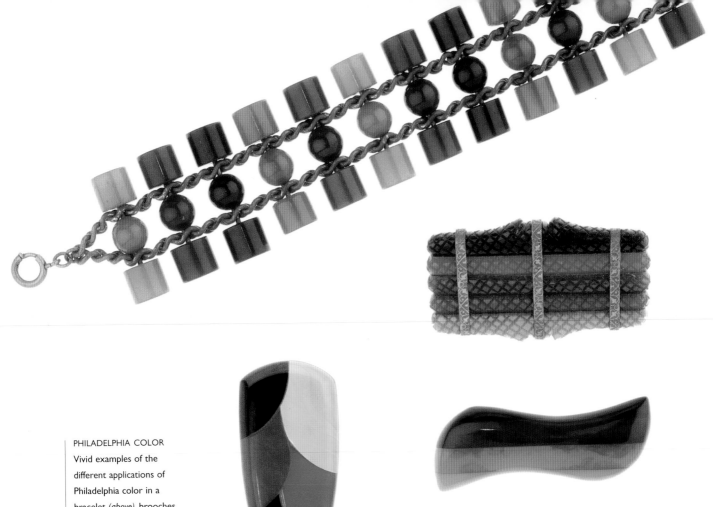

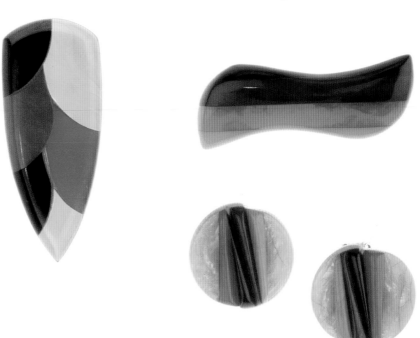

PHILADELPHIA COLOR
Vivid examples of the
different applications of
Philadelphia color in a
bracelet *(above)*, brooches
(right, far right) and
earrings *(bottom)*. Each
piece has a different
sensibility depending
on its shape, carving
and construction.

CARVED BAKELITE

APPLE JUICE NECKLACE
Extraordinarily rare because of its color, this green
Apple Juice Bakelite necklace features a delicate leaf
motif and heavily carved links. Apple Juice pieces were
most commonly crafted in yellow.

CHESS, ANYONE?
Bakelite chessmen
brooches are favorites
of collectors everywhere.
They are painstakingly
carved and are usually
adorned with pearls,
rhinestones and other
decorations. It is very
difficult to collect a
complete set of these
popular pieces because
they were produced in
such small quantities.

UNSIGNED BEAUTIES

These unsigned brooches surpass many signed jewels in their creativity and design. *(Far left)* Set in a sterling vermeil wire frame, the open-back parrot is adorned with clear, red, green and yellow rhinestones and has round, pink, faceted prong-set stones. *(Left)* The 5-inch brass stamped flower features a large, amber marbleized stone at its center.

WILDERNESS WHIMSY
(Top) The sterling-and-rhinestone owl is in a scooped vermeil frame. *(Center)* The elegant gold rabbit sports a red rhinestone eye and four ruby-colored emerald-cut stones. *(Bottom)* Clear rhinestone accents and six pink emerald-cut stones adorn this fanciful elephant.

Signature ELEMENTS

MARCEL BOUCHER (BOUCHER ET CIE)

Marcel Boucher began his career working for Cartier in Paris in the 1910s. From the very first designs, Boucher's jewelry was notable for its superb workmanship in metal, rhinestones and enamel. The quality of the craftsmanship is such that Boucher pieces are often mistaken for precious jewelry.

In the 1920s, Boucher relocated to Cartier's New York studio, where he was employed until the stock market crash of 1929. He continued to work in New York for several costume jewelers, including Mazer Brothers, until he formed his own company, Boucher et Cie, in 1937.

Boucher et Cie was sold in 1972 to an American watch manufacturer.

THE ARTISTRY OF PENNINO BROTHERS

These signature brooches of pink-gold sterling vermeil, set in swirling bow and floral motifs and studded with high-quality stones, are one reason Pennino Brothers' work is considered to be among the finest costume jewelry.

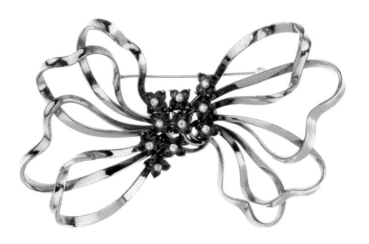

FLORAL BROOCHES

(Above) This ribbon bow features a cluster of prong-set, unfoiled rhinestones. *(Right, top)* A graceful sweep ends in flowers on a filigree setting with faceted pink stones and bezel-set red rhinestones. *(Right)* This dramatic bouquet has bezel-set elevated rhinestones and faceted, open-back amber stones.

DOUBLE FLOWER BOUQUET

This classic Pennino brooch combines bow and floral
motifs in larger-than-life proportions. It is set in sterling
vermeil with layered flowers of prong-set crystals, pink
stones and red cushion-cut stones.

THE SPARKLE OF SILSON AND VOGUE

While Silson is best known for its mass-produced patriotic brooches, the firm also created breathtaking pieces, such as the runway brooch below. Vogue used unfoiled crystals in a way that captured light and gave the jewels life.

SILSON TREMBLER BROOCH
This magnificent gold-and-rhinestone runway brooch is a testimony to Silson's ability to create masterpieces. The flowers, of pavé- and bezel-set rhinestones, are spring-set so they tremble as the wearer moves.

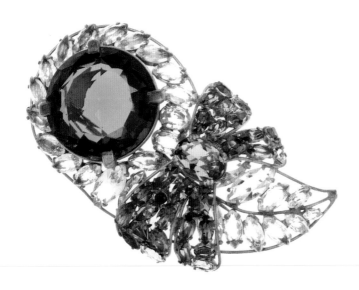

VOGUE BROOCHES

Elaborate bows, with crystals seemingly suspended in air, became the signature style for Vogue brooches of the forties. Each piece below is constructed on a gold-wire frame, with prong-set open-back stones.

CHANEL FIGURALS AND DeROSA BLOOMS

Taking the snobbery out of jewelry, Chanel created a series of fanciful pot-metal and coarsely enameled brooches in animal, floral and bow motifs. American designer DeRosa was known for its well-crafted pieces.

FLIGHTS OF FANCY

(Above, left) The Goofy Frog brooch, with eyes and webbed feet of pavé-set rhinestones, is among the most sought-after Chanel pot-metal pieces. *(Above)* This gold-tone flower has painted enamel leaves and prong-set, navette-cut stones. *(Left)* Simple and pretty, the bow brooch features painted enamel flowers and pavé-set rhinestones. All three brooches are signed.

DeRosa NECKLACE AND BROOCHES
The contrast between the coarser flowers and the
fragile metalwork in this unique design creates an
interesting synergy. These pieces are part of a series
of heavily painted red flowers on well-articulated gold
metal leaves, with translucent green enamel detailing.

THE SIGNATURE STYLE OF WILLIAM HOBÉ

Hobé is celebrated for his intricate use of gold vermeil and sterling in the fashioning of floral masterpieces.

COLLAR NECKLACE
This Baroque-style necklace is an excellent example of Hobé's craftsmanship at its finest. The collar is of sterling silver vermeil with large bezel-set, peridot-colored crystals, unfoiled, with open backs. Each stone is set in an intricate motif of gold leaves and flowers.

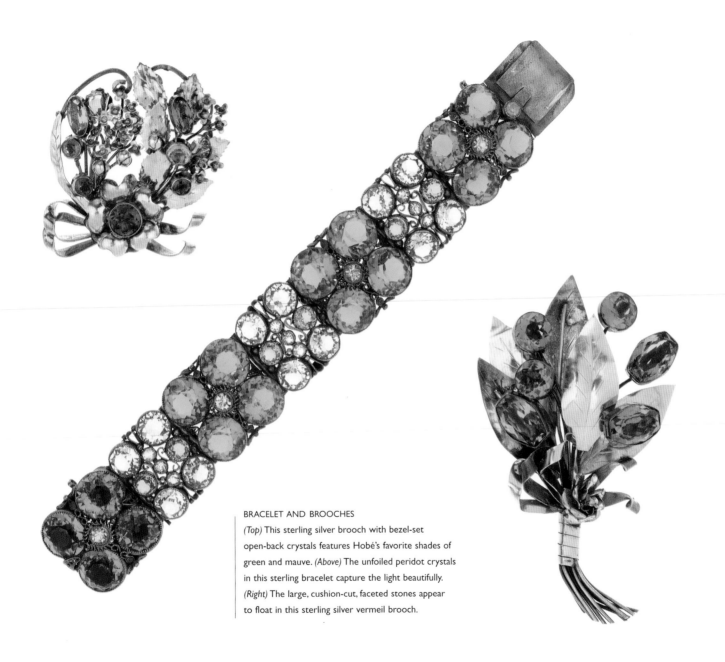

BRACELET AND BROOCHES

(Top) This sterling silver brooch with bezel-set
open-back crystals features Hobé's favorite shades of
green and mauve. *(Above)* The unfoiled peridot crystals
in this sterling bracelet capture the light beautifully.
(Right) The large, cushion-cut, faceted stones appear
to float in this sterling silver vermeil brooch.

HOBÉ FILIGREE AND TRIFARI FANTASY

Early works by Hobé include portrait images and netsuke-type figures, or bandoras. Trifari pieces, prized for their meticulous workmanship, are highly collectible today.

HOBÉ CRYSTAL BROOCHES AND BRACELETS

Each unfoiled crystal in these pieces is bezel-set in a filigreed, hand-formed setting. *(Top, right)* The bracelets feature a remarkable array of crystal cuts—round, teardrop, marquis, cushion, octagon and triangular. *(Bottom, right)* This bandora brooch offers a surprising combination of ivory and multihued crystals.

TRIFARI PARROT BROOCH

No piece demonstrates the artistry and skill of Trifari more beautifully than this rare 5-inch brooch. Note the parrot's extraordinary faceted pink-crystal belly, unfoiled and set in an open back. The head, wings and tail are encrusted with clear rhinestones, baguettes and oval prong-set stones.

Signature ELEMENTS

THE EXCELLENCE OF TRIFARI

Trifari came into prominence as a costume jewelry maker in the 1930s, and its work is among the most sought-after of the period. Chief designer Alfred Philippe had previously worked for Cartier and Van Cleef & Arpels of Paris, and took inspiration from the work of these fine jewelers.

Exquisite taste and impeccable work-manship make Trifari creations very collectible. The enameling on the jewelry is always immaculate, the stones beautifully set tightly together—unlike the coarser pieces mass-produced by many of Trifari's contemporaries using similar materials and techniques.

BRACELET, EARRINGS AND BROOCHES
(Right) This series of pearl-and-enamel jewelry was a Trifari trademark. Note the flowing lines in black enamel and the generous use of pearls.

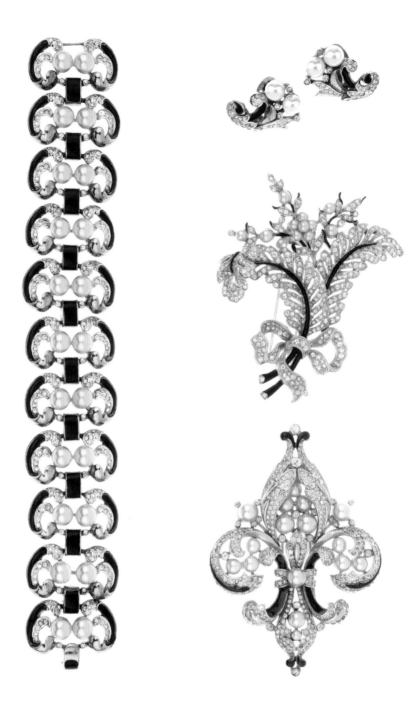

INSPIRED BY CARTIER
These bracelets, designed by Alfred Philippe for Trifari in the 1930s, were inspired by Cartier designs. *(Top)* Half-moon enamel domes are edged with rhinestones and green baguettes. *(Center)* This black enamel bracelet has "fruit salad" stones, which were first made popular by Cartier. The removable clips on either side of the bracelet can be worn as dress clips. *(Bottom)* Similar in materials to the bracelet at the top, this bangle is of curved enamel with rhinestone links.

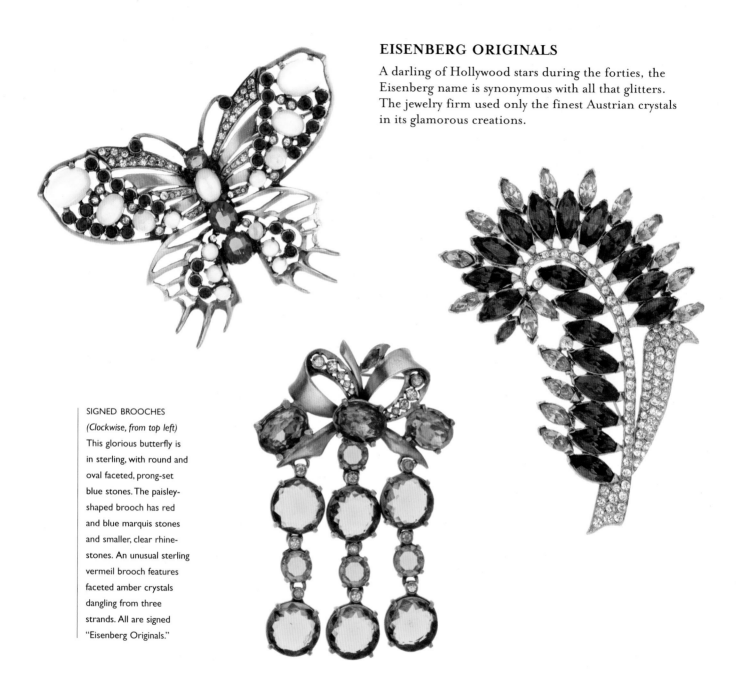

EISENBERG ORIGINALS

A darling of Hollywood stars during the forties, the Eisenberg name is synonymous with all that glitters. The jewelry firm used only the finest Austrian crystals in its glamorous creations.

SIGNED BROOCHES
(Clockwise, from top left)
This glorious butterfly is in sterling, with round and oval faceted, prong-set blue stones. The paisley-shaped brooch has red and blue marquis stones and smaller, clear rhine-stones. An unusual sterling vermeil brooch features faceted amber crystals dangling from three strands. All are signed "Eisenberg Originals."

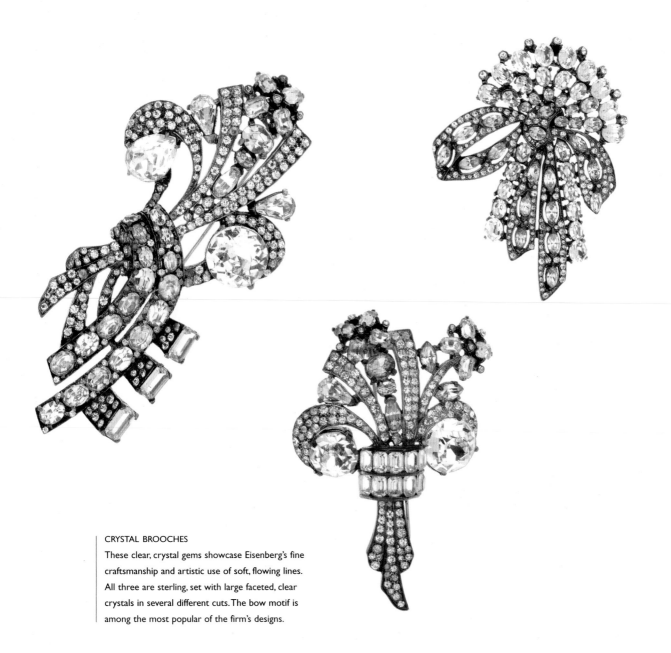

CRYSTAL BROOCHES

These clear, crystal gems showcase Eisenberg's fine
craftsmanship and artistic use of soft, flowing lines.
All three are sterling, set with large faceted, clear
crystals in several different cuts. The bow motif is
among the most popular of the firm's designs.

CORO DUETTES AND BROOCH

Patented in 1930, Coro Duettes were inspired by
Cartier's early dress-clip pairs.

(Above and left) These
charming Duettes can be
worn either as single
brooches or as two separate
clips. They are gold-plated,
with enamel and rhinestone
details. *(Right)* This striking
bird brooch is an impressive
3-inch stylized enamel figural.

(Far left, top) The rose design, of painted green and blue enamel with rhinestone borders, is repeated in the brooch at the top right. (Left) This floral trembler Duette has pistils of small rhinestones. (Far left, bottom) A very rare brooch, this lovely pair of enamel seahorses is accented with pavé-set rhinestones and baguettes.

WHIMSY FOR THE JACKET OR LAPEL

These unsophisticated treasures brought some much-needed
levity during the post-Depression and war years.

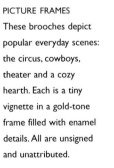

PICTURE FRAMES
These brooches depict
popular everyday scenes:
the circus, cowboys,
theater and a cozy
hearth. Each is a tiny
vignette in a gold-tone
frame filled with enamel
details. All are unsigned
and unattributed.

ROBOTIC FIGURALS
Abstract and ahead of
their time, these animated
figurals are made of
copper-colored and gold-
tone metal with detailed
enameling. Little is known
about the artists who
created them, since
the pieces were very
rarely signed.

SANDOR BROOCHES AND CZECH FIGURALS

<u>Sandor</u>'s enamel brooches are among the most creative designs in costume jewelry. Intricate and lovely, the Czech figural brooches are recognizable by their silver open-grid settings.

SANDOR ENAMEL WIRE BROOCHES
Each of these superbly enameled brooches is in sterling silver decorated with prong-set rhinestones. Fragile and rare, they are all handmade and often feature bow motifs.

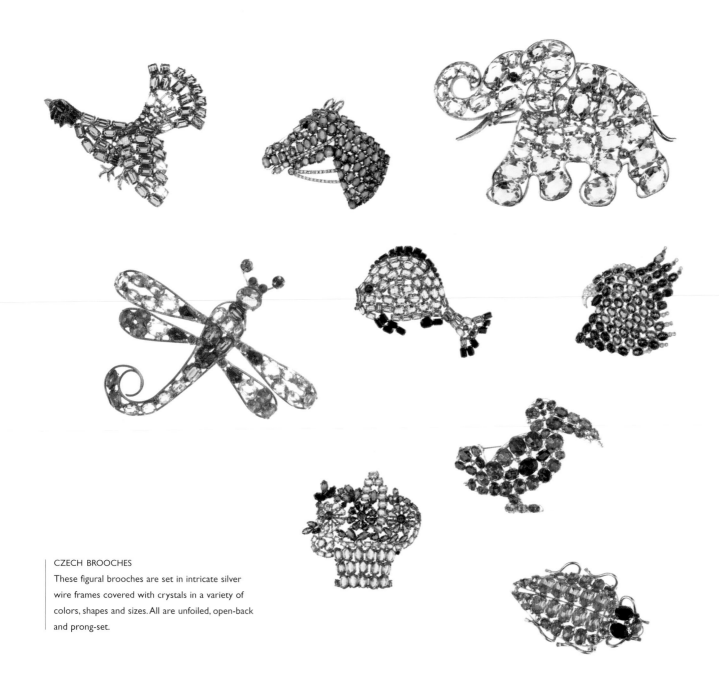

CZECH BROOCHES

These figural brooches are set in intricate silver wire frames covered with crystals in a variety of colors, shapes and sizes. All are unfoiled, open-back and prong-set.

HASKELL ARTISTRY IN BEADS

WIRE BEADED BRACELETS
(Right) This prototype consists of colorful wood beads sewn onto a woven piping covering a wire frame. *(Far right)* The red beaded bracelet is an early wire wrap design that was put into production, making it easier to find than the prototypes. *(Bottom)* A wraparound gunmetal bracelet exemplifies Haskell's facility with combinations of colors and materials. *(Below)* This ultra-feminine bracelet, also a prototype, consists of dozens of small, floral-shaped, blown-glass beads.

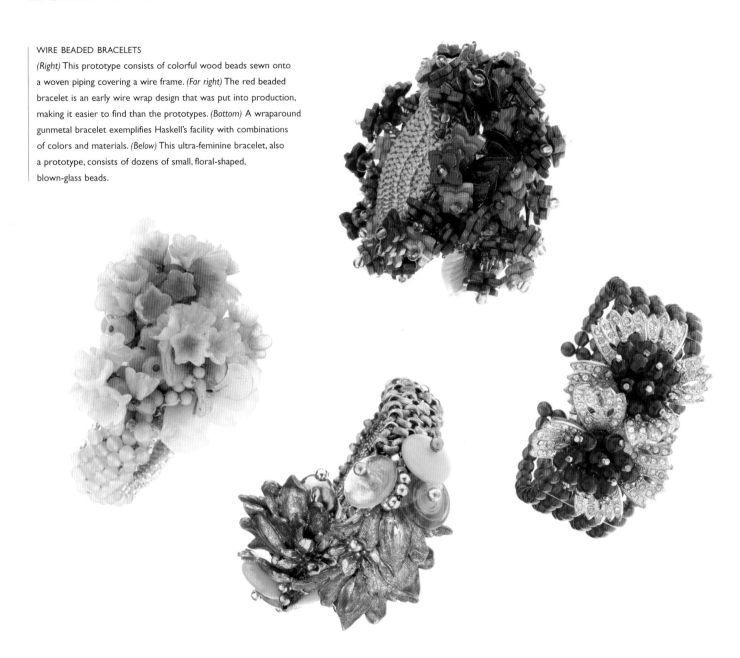

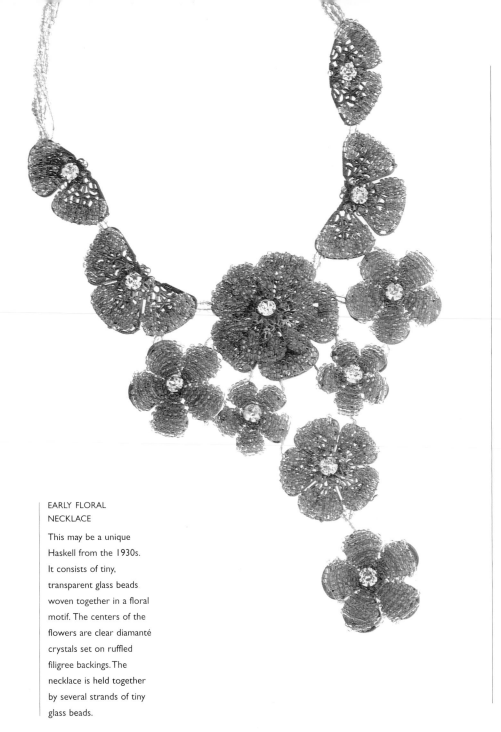

EARLY FLORAL NECKLACE

This may be a unique Haskell from the 1930s. It consists of tiny, transparent glass beads woven together in a floral motif. The centers of the flowers are clear diamanté crystals set on ruffled filigree backings. The necklace is held together by several strands of tiny glass beads.

MIRIAM HASKELL

Shortly after Miriam Haskell opened her first shop in New York City in 1926, she hired Frank Hess as her head of design and a wonderful partnership ensued. Thanks to Haskell's business savvy and Hess's artistic vision, Haskell jewelry quickly found a widespread market.

The hallmark of Haskell jewelry was quality—a corporate commitment that Miriam Haskell insisted on. Pieces were designed to be worn with couture, and Haskell became known for exquisite work with beads and crystal, elaborate filigree and refined wiring.

The elaborate jewelry most associated with Haskell was designed by Frank Hess during his most creative period in the 1950s. After Hess retired in 1960, designers—including Larry Vrba, Robert Clark and Millie Petronzio—continued the legacy of Haskell excellence.

CHANEL POURED-GLASS NECKLACE
Clusters of poured-glass petals fom Maison Gripoix
dangle from the collar of Coco Chanel's striking
necklace in her signature red and green color
combination.

The Fifties

(1950–1959)

OPTIMISTIC, OPULENT, GLAMOROUS

Peace and prosperity reigned in the 1950s, and a sense of security and normalcy replaced the tribulations of the war years. The increasingly popular automobile facilitated outings, and a favorite jaunt was going to the movies. As fashion doyenne Diana Vreeland observed, "For Hollywood, everything was larger than life…. The diamonds were bigger, the furs were thicker…there were miles of bugle beads, diamanté and sequins. Hollywood was paved with glitter, shine and glory." The relationship between celebrity, fashion and faux jewelry was forged during this decade as stars showed allegiance to specific costume jewelry designers, wearing their pieces in films and even appearing as models in their print campaigns. Joan Crawford advertised Miriam Haskell and Joseff of Hollywood. Sonja Henie and Lana Turner touted Napier, and Carole Lombard wore Trifari.

Poise, taste and grooming were the hallmarks of fashion. The confluence of Hollywood glamour, mass production of clothing and jewelry, and greater leisure time softened distinctions between age and socioeconomic class. Each season, manufacturers such as Trifari sent designers to cover the European couture shows to create seasonal looks in jewelry. Magazines advised women to see fashion as a jigsaw puzzle and encouraged them to

SCHIAPARELLI DUCK BROOCH
Elsa Schiaparelli's jewelry from the 1950s is characterized by its bold colors and abstract floral and faunal designs. Here, in a 4-inch dangler brooch, she combines pink and turquoise enamel with bezel-set stones. Note the trio of ducks in profile, each dangling a pearl from its beak. Well made and expensive, Schiaparelli's American work is always signed and is highly collectible.

choose their shoes, handbags, gloves, hats and costume jewelry to complement each ensemble. Taste could not be bought, *Vogue* told its readers, but it could be acquired.

Sparkle now appeared everywhere. It was no longer considered vulgar to wear gems during the day. In fact, women's clothing was often tailored specifically to accommodate the addition of jewelry. Suits were cut with deep breast pockets to welcome brooches; day clothes, such as the ubiquitous twin set, had "bracelet" sleeves that stopped well short of the wrist to better show off rows of bangles; and plunging décolletés invited adornment with a grand parure, dress clips or a dazzling bib necklace.

And because nothing was too much in the 1950s, fashion designers also sewed gems right into the hems, waistbands and sleeves of their creations. Jewels turned up in unexpected places: pins at shirt cuffs; a string of pearls wound around a chignon; a bar brooch along the prominent seam of a suit; a bird pin, ready to take flight, perched high on the shoulder; an asymmetrical rhinestone necklace that draped across the front and dangled tantalizingly in the back. Pins on furs, shoes and handbags! Enormous shimmering tremblant pins with springs shivered with each movement of the wearer.

Fake was chic, and fashionable women were expected to own a range of jewelry—real and faux. Coco Chanel famously said, "Jewelry is not meant to make us look rich; it is meant to adorn." Designers fulfilled the growing demand for "good-humored," brazenly fake conversation pieces by creating extravagant, larger-than-life pins, bracelets, bib or collar necklaces, 4-inch cuffs and shoulder-duster earrings in a range of mediums.

DRAGONFLY BROOCH
New York jeweler Henry Schreiner used paste stones, inverted crystals and diamanté in unusual color combinations. This 4-inch brooch features two unfoiled, elongated, faceted crystals.

Christian Dior, in collaboration with Swarovski, created the aurora borealis stone. A polychrome metallic coating gave this gem a beguiling iridescent quality, echoing the style of the eighteenth-century French court of which Dior was so fond. (Today, the aurora borealis stone is used by Dior in the bottle for Pure Poison perfume.) Manufacturers were always on the lookout for new stones and colors, and many had exclusive rights to use them. For example, Francis Winter, who created jewels for many European couturiers, was given the rights to Swarovski crystals in Bermuda Blue, Heliotrope and a bluish-mauve stone called Volcanique; Madame Gripoix had permission to use yellow stones, and Roger Jean-Pierre had access to a unique flower-cut stone. Pearls also remained a strong force, particularly in the mid-fifties, as they accessorized the Little Black Dress. They came in a range of shades—champagne, coffee, lemon yellow, cream, gray—meant to enhance each complexion and ensemble.

America in the 1950s, with its ethos of "Buy the new, discard the old," gave a huge boon to the costume jewelry industry. European designers still made small-production, high-quality couture pieces, but U.S. factories cranked out sparkling gems at modest prices for millions of consumers. New designers Har, Rebajes, Bartek and Bergère joined the ranks of top-tier manufacturers like Boucher, Coro, Trifari and Haskell, now in their most creative periods.

SIGNATURE HASKELL

This elaborate six-strand crystal bracelet with floral motif features the gilt metal leaves and flat-backed rose montée stones that are hallmarks of Miriam Haskell's innovative designs. She and her head designers traveled the world to find the best materials, such as these crystals from Austria.

During the 1950s, Miriam Haskell, who was the first costume jeweler to have her own storefront in the late thirties, produced popular cluster beadwork in custom-made Japanese pearls and carved glass. Her pieces were copied by big manufacturers such as Corocraft, as well as by her own designers Robert DeMario and another colleague named Eugene. There were several lesser-known designers, including Amourelle and Jonné, who did similar work. (As I mentioned earlier, I was lucky enough to purchase several gorgeous prototype beadwork pieces that showcase Haskell's flair.)

In a savvy business move in 1955, Christian Dior hired a German manufacturer to produce a range of seasonal costume jewelry for the House of Dior. The designer, who also controlled the marketing and display of the jewels (thus reinforcing his brand identity), inspired many couturiers to follow his lead. Many excellent designers worked for Dior—including Roger Scemama, Kramer, Mitchell Maer, Coppola e Toppo, Roger Jean-Pierre, Madame Gripoix, Paco Rabanne, as well as one of my favorites, Henry Schreiner.

Schreiner opened his own company in New York in 1951. He is known for his unusual settings, using open prongs that cap his stones. He also set stones in an inverted position, with the pointed end up, which created dazzling prismatic effects. Schreiner's signature stone cut was the keystone, or kite-shaped stone, which he employed to create undulations in his most beautiful works, the ruffle pins. He was not afraid to use different combinations of colors and stones, giving his work tremendous excitement. Another designer who favored bold compositions in the 1950s was William Hobé; his dramatic parures were worn by many Hollywood stars, including Bette Davis and Ava Gardner.

This charming print ad for her perfume Shocking is quintessential Elsa Schiaparelli—a playful take on an outdoor scene by Marcel Vertes.

At this time, a little-known designer by the name of Gustave Sherman was venturing to the fashion shows in Paris and New York, and creating his own statement pieces in Montreal, Canada. His enormous rhinestone cuffs—made with bold-hued, elongated marquise- and round-cut rhinestones in highly polished rhodium settings—came with a lifetime guarantee. His grandson tells the amusing story of a client who called the Sherman home to tell him that her bangle had fallen into the kitchen garburetor. She wanted the jeweler to replace it, since it came with a lifetime warranty. To his wife's chagrin, Sherman did replace the bracelet, telling his wife, "If someone wants my piece enough to call me, she deserves to have it." Sherman's work is becoming better known outside Canada and his pieces are now quite collectible.

Elsa Schiaparelli continued to create her fanciful couture, prêt-à-porter and jewelry lines in France. However, after the departure in 1951 of Hubert de Givenchy (who had designed her popular boutique collection), losses from the couture business mounted. In 1954, Schiaparelli packed her bags for New York to concentrate on creating faux jewels with DeRosa

ROBERT SIGNED ORIGINAL
Best known for pearl and gold cluster jewelry and natural motifs, designer Robert Levy created a diverse body of work. This bracelet is composed of three oval, cabochon, prong-set stones in japanned metal, accented with faceted crystals, also prong-set, in various shapes— baguette, square, round and navette. Robert jewelry is usually marked.

manufacturers, who continued to produce Schiaparelli jewelry until 1970. Her high-volume 1950s pieces—with moon rocks, aurora borealis stones and jelly beans—employ an audacious combination of colors, motifs and elements. There was never anything modest about Schiaparelli, and that is why we love her!

Ironically, Schiaparelli's last couture collection, on February 3, 1954, was followed only two days later by the return of archrival Coco Chanel after a fifteen-year absence from fashion. The seventy-one-year-old Chanel's collection was poorly received at her 31 rue Cambon salon. "We watched the mannequins file by in icy silence," wrote journalist Michel Déon. Although Chanel managed to recover from the debacle (this was critical in light of the fortunes at stake in her branded perfumes), the Youthquake movement of the 1960s could already be heard amid the genteel tinkling of teacups.

CHRISTIAN DIOR BROOCH
This signed brooch of delicate pavé on rhodium-backed metal with pearl danglers displays Dior's fine workmanship. Variations of the design have also appeared in precious jewelry, making this a true crossover piece.

HOLLYCRAFT SIGNED BRACELET
Hollycraft was in its heyday in the 1950s, when its intricate designs often echoed the Victorian style. (Right) Typical of Hollycraft's colorful, tightly set jewelry, this bracelet has rhinestones of various hues and shapes prong-set on japanned backing. Most Hollycraft pieces are signed and dated.

RARE FRENCH CLASSICS

These charming unsigned French necklaces, most likely designed by either Louis Rousselet or Robert Piguet in the early fifties, are rarely found today because of their fragility and the limited production quantities.

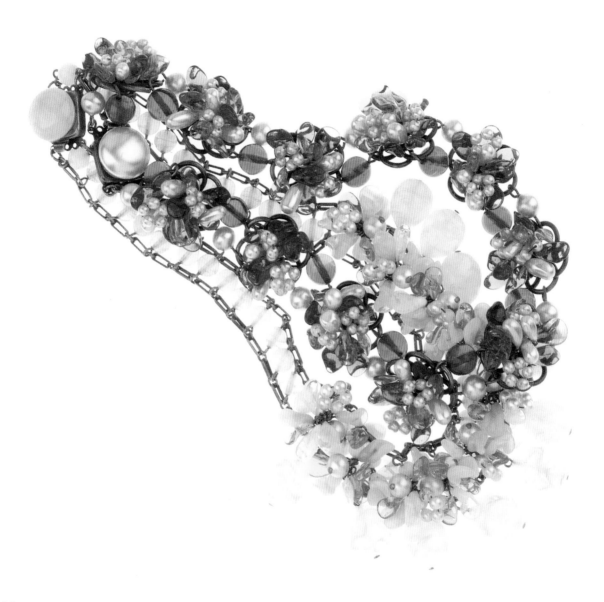

(*Above*) The back of this necklace is almost as beautiful as the front. Note the classic sterling "rosebud" construction. (*Below*) The double-chain necklace has translucent pink beads between its ladder rails and poured-glass bead danglers.

SIGNATURE PIECES BY HASKELL

Leaves, flowers and other motifs from nature
are recurring themes in Miriam Haskell's
complex designs.

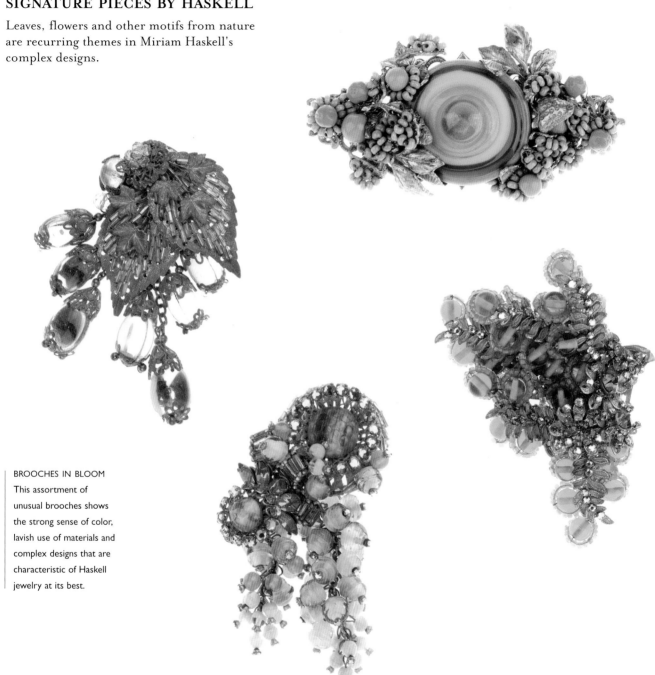

BROOCHES IN BLOOM
This assortment of
unusual brooches shows
the strong sense of color,
lavish use of materials and
complex designs that are
characteristic of Haskell
jewelry at its best.

NECKLACE AND BRACELET

Note the beautiful and unusual color combination and the repeated use of the floral motif on the central medallion and clasp of the five-strand bracelet *(above)* and the four-strand necklace. The hook clasp, with small bead clusters, is signed "Miriam Haskell." Her clasps were often elaborate.

HASKELL PEARL JEWELRY
After the Second World War, Miriam Haskell used white, pink, brown and gray faux pearls from Japan for their deep, lustrous finish. Pearls from this era are now difficult to find in their original condition. *(Right)* The long, heavy necklace with prong-set stones is a prototype from Eli and Sandy Moss's collection. *(Below)* The shoulder brooch was meant to be worn draped front and back over a shoulder. *(Far right)* The flat-edged brooch was worn like a medal, high on the chest.

UNSIGNED BEAUTY
This elaborate French poured-glass collar necklace,
possibly by Maison Gripoix for Chanel, has unusual
cut and carved glass beads in the shape of leaves and
"melon balls" at the ends of each strand. A piece
like this is very rare.

INSPIRED BY HASKELL

Although Amourelle jewelry was created in the early sixties
by former Haskell chief designer Frank Hess, the pieces were
definitely inspired by his artistry at Haskell during the fifties.
Jonné costume jewelry is also often mistaken for Haskell's
because of the richness of its materials and design.

AMOURELLE BROOCHES

These beautifully rendered flowers show similarities
to Haskell's brooches. Note the clusters of different-
colored stones on gold-filigree backs. Few examples
of this magnificent jewelry are found today. Amourelle
jewelry is signed in a heart-shaped brass plaque, as
shown at right.

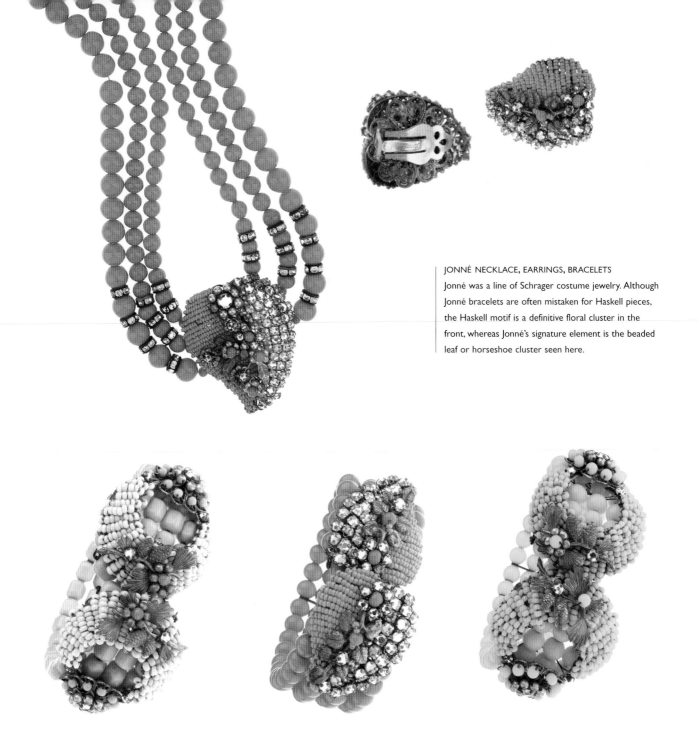

JONNÉ NECKLACE, EARRINGS, BRACELETS
Jonné was a line of Schrager costume jewelry. Although Jonné bracelets are often mistaken for Haskell pieces, the Haskell motif is a definitive floral cluster in the front, whereas Jonné's signature element is the beaded leaf or horseshoe cluster seen here.

Signature ELEMENTS

ROBERT DeMARIO

Robert DeMario founded his company
in New York City in 1945 and it continued
to thrive into the 1960s. The firm quickly
earned a reputation for its clusters of
glass beads, pearls and rhinestones on
gilt filigree.

DeMario jewelry is prized for the
boldness of its designs and for its inventive
use of color. Although DeMario creations
are sometimes confused with Haskell's
because of the intricacy of the beadwork
and pearl designs, the DeMario style is
distinctive, with faceted Austrian crystal
beads and rhinestones.

The company's production quantities
were very small, which makes DeMario
jewelry highly collectible.

DeMARIO EARRINGS,
BROOCH AND BRACELET
It is easy to see why
DeMario's work is often
mistaken for Haskell's—
the sensibilities are very
similar, as seen in these
pieces, although the
constructions are
different. *(Above)* The
brooch and matching
earrings are gilt metal
filigree studded with tiny
prong-set rhinestones.
(Left) This fancy wired
crystal bracelet has
DeMario's signature
beaded cluster on
the front.

ROBERT JEWELRY—DESIGNS BY ROBERT LEVY

Robert, originally a trademark of the Fashioncraft Jewelry Company of New York, changed its name to Robert Originals, Inc., in 1960.

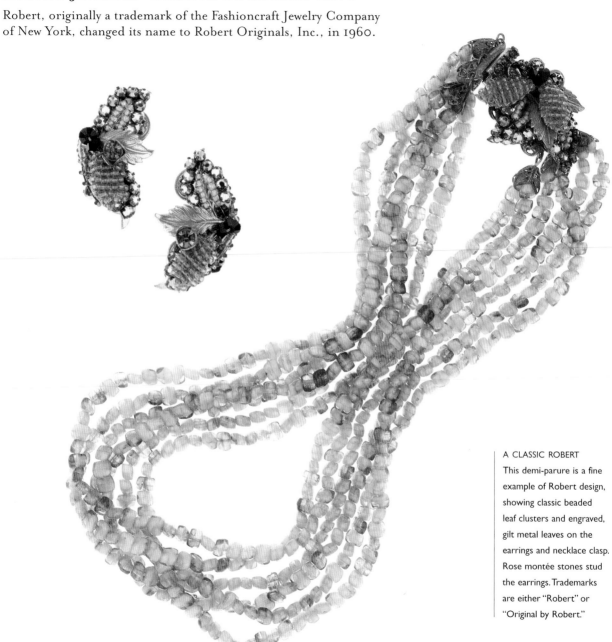

A CLASSIC ROBERT
This demi-parure is a fine example of Robert design, showing classic beaded leaf clusters and engraved, gilt metal leaves on the earrings and necklace clasp. Rose montée stones stud the earrings. Trademarks are either "Robert" or "Original by Robert."

SCHREINER OF NEW YORK

Henry Schreiner was a master designer of costume
jewelry for Trigère and Norelle before he joined Dior
in the late 1940s.

PARURE IN BLUES AND GREENS
Schreiner is known for his unconventional settings,
unusual color combinations and unique stones, such
as the oval purple cabochons, turquoise square-cut
stones and deep-blue round cabochons of this parure.
A Schreiner parure like this is very rare.

WIRE BROOCHES
These are beautiful examples of Schreiner's extravagance in design and his discerning stone selection. The brooches echo the shape and design of Victorian jewelry. *(Top)* The "bush" pin has a gilt wire backing with prong-set pink and purple rhinestones.

SCHREINER IN MILLEFIORI AND COLOR

The millefiori brooches are hard to come by today. They were made with large Venetian glass stones in conjunction with complementary colored stones.

MILLEFIORI BROOCHES
(Far right, bottom) The unique pin with carved green mosaic disks, painted accents and a pale pink, swirled-glass, teardrop dangle is not millefiori, but it is typical of Schreiner design, with its characteristic dome shape. *(Right)* The ruffle pin has keystone-cut crystals in a prong-set matrix. *(Bottom)* These brooches have millefiori glass and prong-set cut stones.

PRONG-SET BROOCHES
This array shows the
diverse color combinations
Schreiner employed to
gorgeous effect. *(Far right,
top)* Sparkling pendaloque-
shaped tiger's-eye stones
are bordered by turquoise
prong-set stones to match
the huge oval cabochon.
(Bottom) The domed stones
and large triangular prongs
of these beauties are
Schreiner signature
elements.

SCHREINER JEWELRY: DAZZLING, DIVERSE AND IN DEMAND

RUFFLES AND BOLD COLOR

Among Schreiner's most coveted gems are his ruffle brooches *(left)*. He was the first designer to use keystones, or layered, kite-shaped crystals, resulting in a ruffled effect. Note the hook-and-eye construction on the reverse side of the brooch, another Schreiner signature. *(Above)* The bracelet, and the matching earrings at left, have turquoise stones and are set in large cup prongs. They, too, exemplify the boldness of color so often seen in Schreiner jewelry.

BRILLIANT BROOCH SETS

These treasures exemplify Schreiner's genius. Note
how the pear-shaped stones, large and unfoiled, are set
so that they capture the light. The translucent, citrine
open-back pendaloque stones in the bottom pieces
are prong-set in gold-tone metal. The carved leaves
are carnelian-colored.

ELSA SCHIAPARELLI

"Schiap," as Elsa Schiaparelli is known to her many devotees, had a love of natural forms, light and fantasy gemstones, which she used to great effect in her highly stylized designs.

CARVED LEAF SET

This necklace and bracelet of carved frosted glass in two shades of gray feature one of Schiaparelli's favorite motifs—the leaf. They are accented with citrine crystals on a japanned backing. The effect is both geometric and quietly elegant.

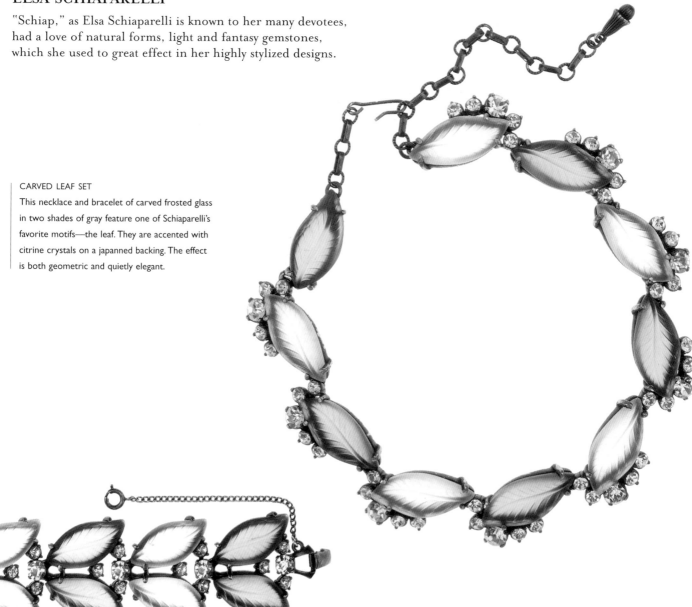

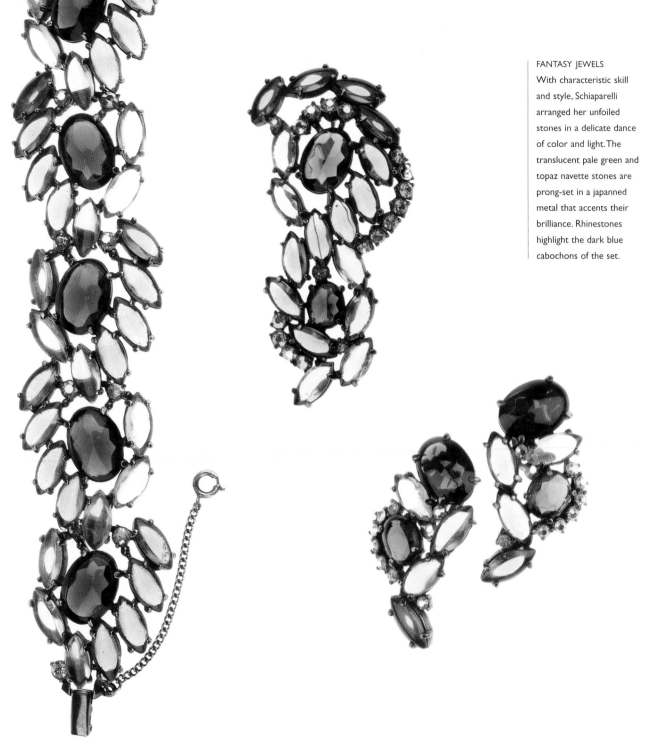

With characteristic skill
and style, Schiaparelli
arranged her unfoiled
stones in a delicate dance
of color and light. The
translucent pale green and
topaz navette stones are
prong-set in a japanned
metal that accents their
brilliance. Rhinestones
highlight the dark blue
cabochons of the set.

Signature ELEMENTS

ELSA SCHIAPARELLI

Born in Rome, Schiaparelli opened her first couture house in Paris in the 1920s and quickly became a rival of Coco Chanel. While both women believed costume jewelry was an art form that deserved recognition, their interpretations of that art form were radically different. Chanel's designs were classic and elegant; Schiaparelli favored exotic designs and bold use of color, especially her signature shocking pink.

Schiaparelli's inspiration came from her friends in the Surrealism art movement. In 1954, she immigrated to New York and began creating audacious jewelry using unusual stones, such as her distinctive moon rocks and watermelon stones.

Schiap's legacy of flamboyant design makes her work a favorite of collectors.

BALL-AND-CHAIN PARURE
Theatrical and chic, this modern design reveals Schiaparelli's interest in Surrealism. It consists of flexible gold snake chains that end in pavé rhinestone balls.

FOILED CRYSTAL SET
Unusual crystals—foiled,
multifaceted, oval and
watermelon-colored—
create a sensational
evening parure. Schiaparelli
used varying types of
watermelon stones in
her jewelry.

THE FIFTIES 129

THE SCHIAPARELLI PALETTE

VARIATIONS ON A THEME
Schiaparelli's jewelry is a
unique play of stonework;
color and crystals tell the
story. She uses a very
simple framework but
achieves interest by the
juxtaposition of pear-
shaped and octagonal
stones. Prong-set aurora
borealis rhinestones
add sparkle.

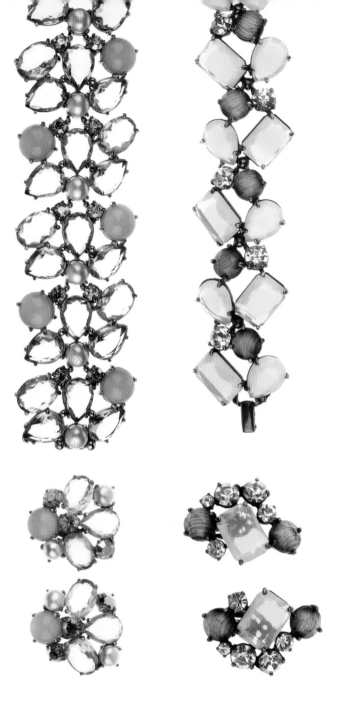

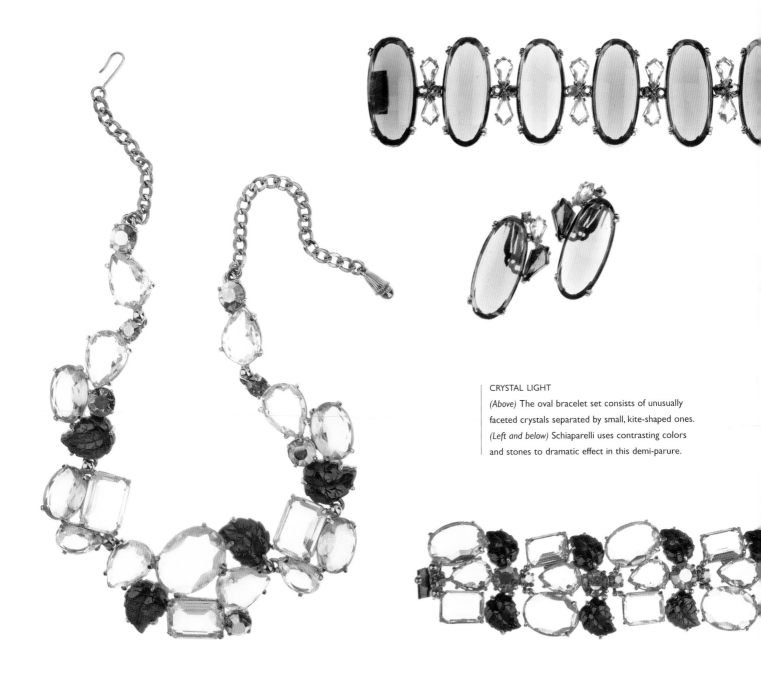

CRYSTAL LIGHT

(Above) The oval bracelet set consists of unusually faceted crystals separated by small, kite-shaped ones. *(Left and below)* Schiaparelli uses contrasting colors and stones to dramatic effect in this demi-parure.

Signature ELEMENTS

GUSTAVE SHERMAN

Gustave Sherman was the son of first-generation immigrants to Canada who had fled Eastern Europe to escape persecution. His interest in jewelry stemmed from an early job as a jewelry salesman. Although he had no formal training, he opened a small manufacturing company, Sherman Costume Jewelry, in Montreal in 1947. By the 1950s, the company was thriving and Sherman was Canada's most recognized costume jeweler.

The company slogan was "Made to last a lifetime" and Sherman was a stickler for high quality—both in workmanship and in the stones he used, many of them Swarovski crystals. He especially loved elongated marquis crystals and often set them as accents in distinctive monochromatic color schemes.

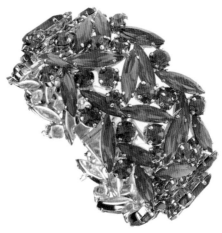

SHERMAN GLITTER
The wide bracelets and cuffs are among the most collectible of Sherman's designs. Note the elongated marquis crystal in both the flat bracelet *(above)* and the red cuff *(right)*. Collectors seek the deep red pieces on japanned backing.

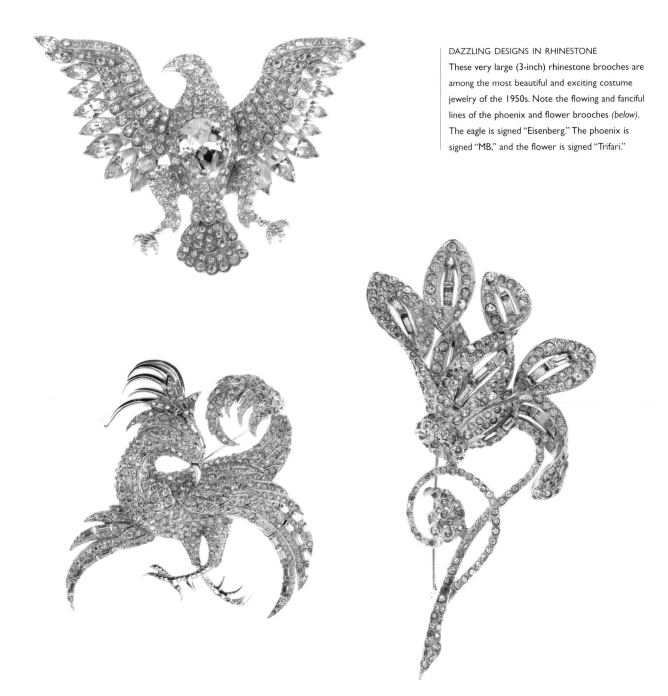

These very large (3-inch) rhinestone brooches are among the most beautiful and exciting costume jewelry of the 1950s. Note the flowing and fanciful lines of the phoenix and flower brooches (below). The eagle is signed "Eisenberg." The phoenix is signed "MB," and the flower is signed "Trifari."

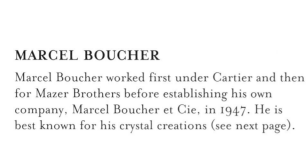

MARCEL BOUCHER

Marcel Boucher worked first under Cartier and then for Mazer Brothers before establishing his own company, Marcel Boucher et Cie, in 1947. He is best known for his crystal creations (see next page).

CHRYSOPRASE NECKLACE

A design departure for Boucher, this innovative necklace has "atomic" projections of gold spikes that are complemented by smooth green squares. The detail above, seen from the back, shows a link that can be used to extend the necklace's length.

These necklaces could easily be mistaken for the
"real thing" because of their exquisite execution
and choice of crystals. Boucher drew inspiration
from the designs of Cartier and Van Cleef & Arpels.
Note the ornate, encrusted rhinestone clasps.

HAR, MAZER BROTHERS AND JOMAZ

Little is known of Har or of his New York company, Hargo, but the jewelry that exists is imaginative and artistically conceived. Mazer Brothers was founded in New York City in 1927. Joseph Mazer started his own line, Jomaz, in 1946.

HAR DRAGON PARURE

This is one of the best known designs in costume jewelry. Avant-garde and theatrical, it pairs green enameling with ruby, turquoise and aurora borealis rhinestones and fantasy-colored moon rocks. Much of Har's work consisted of figurals such as this.

MAZER BROTHERS BRACELET AND EARRINGS/ JOMAZ BRACELET SET

Mazer Brothers and Jomaz creations often were affordable versions of the great designs in precious jewelry. *(Right and far right)* The Jomaz set of brooch, earrings and bracelet has leaves of pavé-set rhinestones and stunning jade cabochons. *(Below)* These Mazer Brothers pendant earrings are of pavé-set crystal rhinestones and green glass, as is the matching bracelet.

SELRO, LERU AND PIERRE

Selro was well known for his brightly colored, molded plastic warriors and devil-face motifs. Leru designs often featured pale pastel stones with delicate metal bases; the lightness was meant to complement summer fashions. Pierre was a Canadian designer whose handmade jewelry is similar to some of the Juliana designs.

SELRO TREASURES

Similar in sensibility to the works of Schiaparelli and Schreiner, this green bracelet set is bold and beautiful. There is a wonderful contrast between the large rectangular stones and the organic and teardrop-shaped accents. A black flower in the center of each link softens the design.

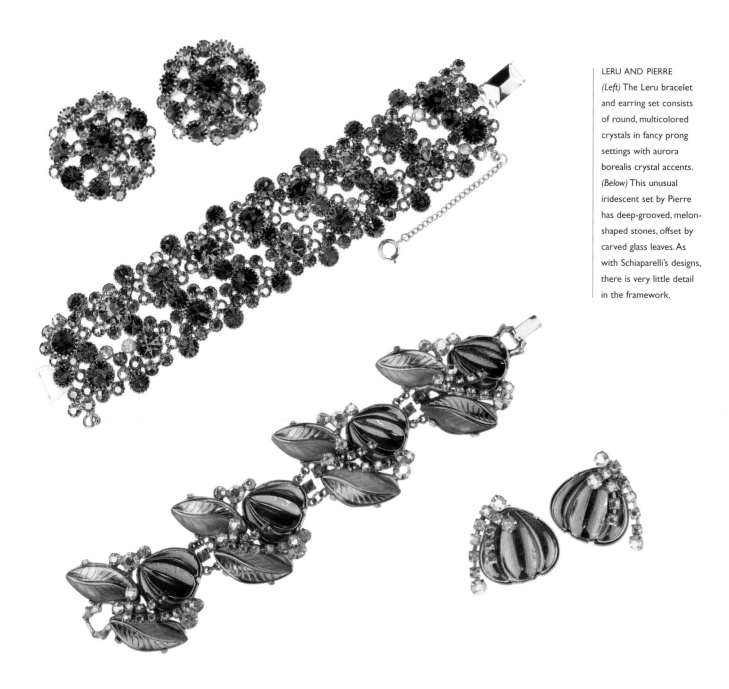

(Left) The Leru bracelet
and earring set consists
of round, multicolored
crystals in fancy prong
settings with aurora
borealis crystal accents.
(Below) This unusual
iridescent set by Pierre
has deep-grooved, melon-
shaped stones, offset by
carved glass leaves. As
with Schiaparelli's designs,
there is very little detail
in the framework.

UNSIGNED WORKS OF ART

Unsigned jewelry is often overlooked by collectors, yet many pieces are both beautiful and unusual. The jewelry was often made to order but was sometimes sold in department stores under each store's own label.

It's still possible to find gorgeous jewels of outstanding craftsmanship among unsigned pieces—including the unfoiled, open-back brooch in "atomic style" *(far right, top)*, with its prong-set trapezoidal stones.

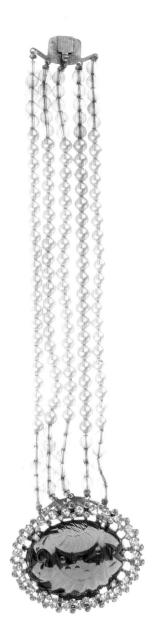

These three wonderful bracelets from the 1950s illustrate the bold style of the era. *(Right)* The bracelet with the large green stone is in a Victorian Revival style, but it is also absolutely contemporary. *(Center)* This bracelet is classic fifties design. *(Far right)* This five-strand bracelet was designed in the style of precious jewelry.

BOLD AND BEAUTIFUL

Much effort was put into the design and construction of these unsigned heavy and three-dimensional bracelets. They were conceived by artistic talents, perhaps for the fashion runway, where bold statements were necessary to match the exaggeration of haute couture collections.

MOTHER-OF-PEARL SHOWSTOPPER

This over-the-top parure is Victorian Revival, with flat, half-moon shells as the focal point. It is rare to find a complete parure in this style.

ALICE CAVINESS AND HATTIE CARNEGIE

Both these designers shone during the fifties. Alice Caviness was known for her big, bold pieces. And Hattie Carnegie wowed Hollywood stars with her feminine, glamorous designs.

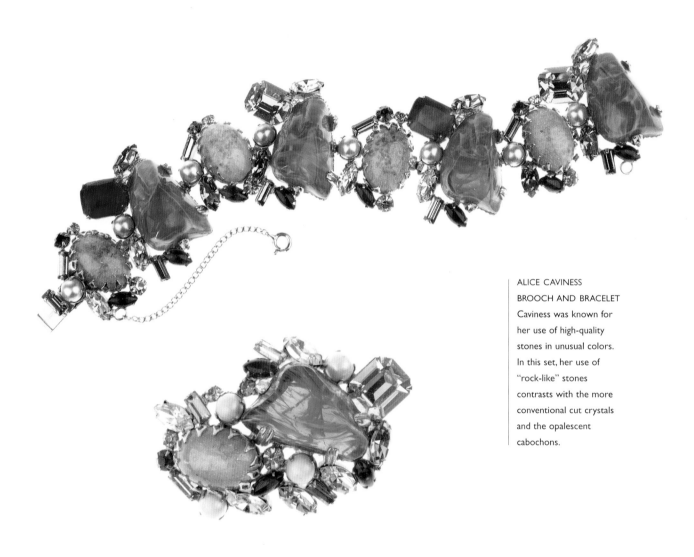

ALICE CAVINESS
BROOCH AND BRACELET
Caviness was known for
her use of high-quality
stones in unusual colors.
In this set, her use of
"rock-like" stones
contrasts with the more
conventional cut crystals
and the opalescent
cabochons.

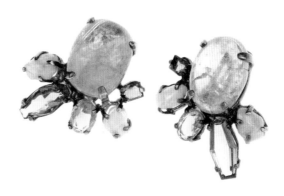

HATTIE CARNEGIE PARURE

Carnegie's favored materials of faux pearls,
rhinestones and glass are featured in this pale,
delicate parure with its double strand of luster
pearls and a large cluster pendant of rose quartz,
and purple and citrine faceted prong-set stones.
Like Chanel, Carnegie first designed costume
jewelry to complement her fashions.

A SPLASH OF COLOR
This is a wonderfully
designed unsigned parure,
set with pink and green
stones. Note the fancy
filigree overlay that
caps the stones.

William Hobé's creations were favored by the
film and theater worlds and were always expensive.
This elegant parure, with its clusters of aquamarine
prong-set stones in silver metal, has pearl and
aurora borealis accents and large iridescent
aqua cabochons.

FRENCH BEADED COLLAR SET
This opulent and richly colored collar consists of
rows of beads strung in overlapping rows. Faux
pearls provide a quiet contrast to the vibrant
glass beads.

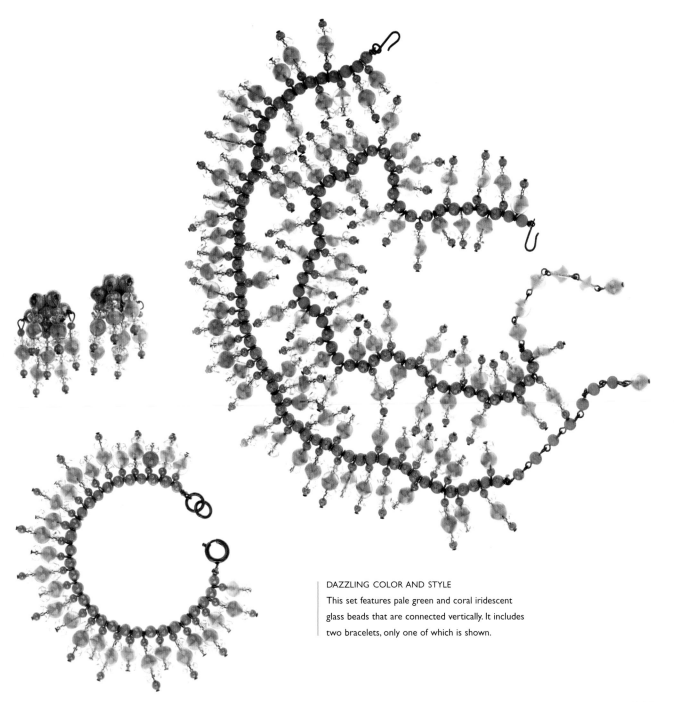

DAZZLING COLOR AND STYLE
This set features pale green and coral iridescent
glass beads that are connected vertically. It includes
two bracelets, only one of which is shown.

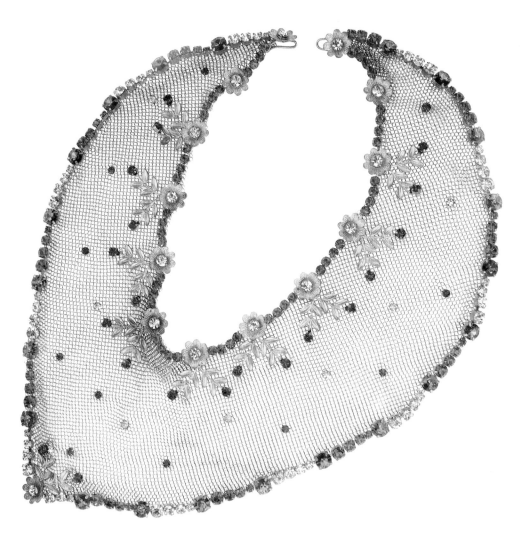

MESH NECKLACE

Of exceptional quality, this mesh necklace embroidered with stones was probably commissioned privately. Its asymmetrical design allows the modified point to fall to the side when it is in place on the neck.

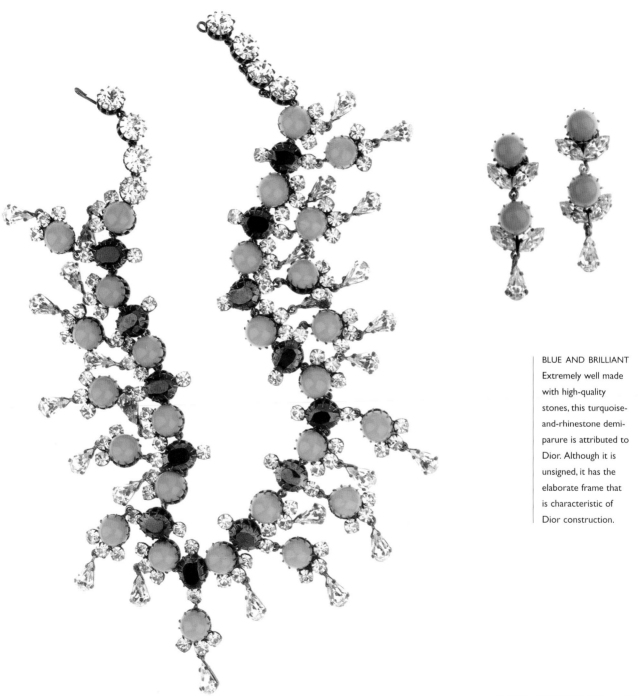

BLUE AND BRILLIANT
Extremely well made
with high-quality
stones, this turquoise-
and-rhinestone demi-
parure is attributed to
Dior. Although it is
unsigned, it has the
elaborate frame that
is characteristic of
Dior construction.

RUNWAY JEWELRY

It is fitting to close this chapter of high glamour with some of the most coveted items of costume jewelry—the runway pieces. These jewels prove that costume pieces can rival precious jewelry in the artistry of their design.

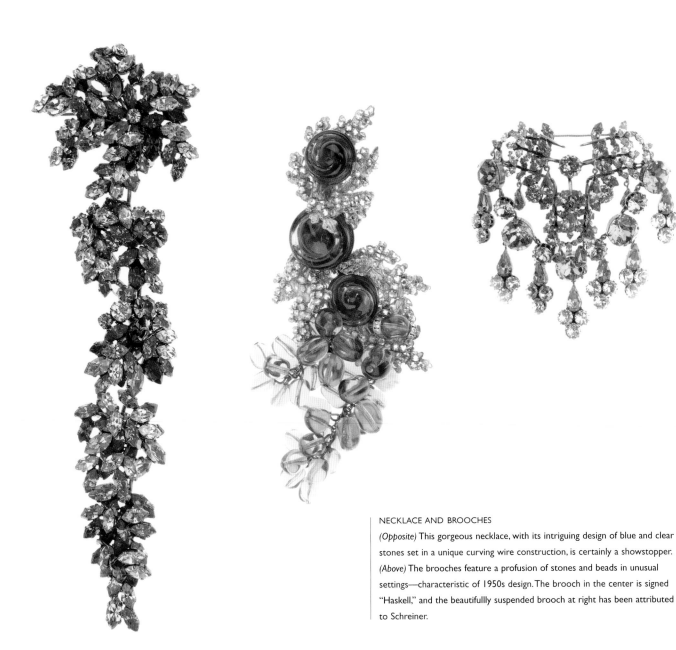

NECKLACE AND BROOCHES

(Opposite) This gorgeous necklace, with its intriguing design of blue and clear stones set in a unique curving wire construction, is certainly a showstopper. *(Above)* The brooches feature a profusion of stones and beads in unusual settings—characteristic of 1950s design. The brooch in the center is signed "Haskell," and the beautifullly suspended brooch at right has been attributed to Schreiner.

FLORAL DRAMA
IN GLASS

The blue poured-glass
petals of this necklace
are strung on wire
so that the branches
are flexible. With
its stunning accent
rhinestones and
free-form design, this
is a unique objet d'art.

INSPIRED BY EGYPT

This poured-glass necklace set is possibly by
Chanel, although it is unsigned. Made of elongated,
turquoise glass lozenges set with rhinestones and
ruby-colored stones, it is both bold and elegant.
Note the keychain link.

This fabulous fuchsia necklace consists of prong-set crystals of many shapes. The stones are set so that the central part of the necklace is slightly dome-shaped. It is a dazzling example of costume jewelry.

A SCULPTED JEWEL
Because of the unusual
construction, the top
layer of crystals in this
necklace forms domes
while the grapes lie
flat. This is considered
a sculptural shape in
jewelry design and this
example, attributed to
"CIS," is a true work
of art.

END-OF-DAY COLLAR
It is said that end-of-day collars were so named because they contain so many different stones, which suggests that the artist used whatever was left over in the workroom at the end of the day. True or not, this example has a beautiful range of colors that lend a festive air to the necklace.

Although this necklace is unsigned, it is very
possibly a Schreiner. The remarkable contrast of
gunmetal with garnet red, set in a lacy, complex
design, makes this one of the costume greats.

COPPOLA E TOPPO

The Italian brother-and-sister team of Coppola e Toppo designed for such greats as Valentino, Pucci and Balenciaga. Their signature jewels include elaborately woven collars with tightly wrapped and clustered beads. Coppola e Toppo designs are still among the most sought-after and expensive costume jewelry.

The Sixties
& Seventies

(1960–1979)

ARTISANAL, PERMISSIVE, GLOBAL

If the 1950s were all about the celebration of haute bourgeois values, the following decade smashed social conventions like a hammer against glass. The epicenter of the Swinging Sixties was Carnaby Street in London. It was the fount of counterculture pop music, film, art and fashion. The era's new aristocracy included hairdressers, pop stars, supermodels, photographers and fashion designers. The Pill, the moon landing, the Kennedys, the revolt against the Vietnam War… Suddenly, the established order was flipped upside down. Feminine and ladylike styles gave way to space-age, unisex and mod fashion trends. British designer Mary Quant created a revolution with the launch of the miniskirt, the trouser suit, hot pants and vinyl clothing. Hairstylist Vidal Sassoon created bold, geometric haircuts, such as the Five-Point Cut. A quartet of skinny, leggy, sassy models—Twiggy, Penelope Tree, Veruschka and Jean Shrimpton—vied with Jacqueline Kennedy and Audrey Hepburn for the role of sixties style icon.

The sexual revolution not only loosened social behavior, it also anointed new erogenous zones. Up-dos and kicky short haircuts revealed the ears and the neck—a bareness that cried out for long, dramatic earrings. Kenneth Jay Lane, the Detroit-born designer, began his career making shoes for Dior and Delman. He also worked as the creative director at Hattie Carnegie before becoming a costume jewelry impresario in the sixties, launching his career with a collection of large, rhinestone-encrusted, plastic earrings. The lightweight materials allowed him to create jewels so massive that some of his clients had to use spirit gum in order to keep them on through the evening. His creations were embraced by socialites and by actresses

Elizabeth Taylor and Audrey Hepburn, who wore his pieces alongside their fine jewelry. Lane recounted that at one pre-Oscar party in Los Angeles, Hepburn approached Taylor and inquired whether her earrings were KJL. "No," replied Taylor, "they're 'Richard Burton.'"

Lane still produces today and his gems have been worn by several first ladies, including Barbara Bush, who accessorized her Arnold Scaasi gown with Lane's three-strand pearl choker at the Inaugural Ball. In the 1970s, when New York socialite Nan Kempner was robbed of her substantial jewelry collection, she reputedly called Lane the next day and said, "I'll take a dozen of everything."

Although the hellion-like sixties did not officially begin until 1964 with the Beatles' arrival in America, once the decade ignited, there was no turning back. Couture, once the apex of chic, was now considered matronly. Fashionable young women moved as far from their mothers' choice of attire as possible by embracing a brave new wave of edgy looks from designers Pierre Cardin, Paco Rabanne, Giorgio di Sant'Angelo, Courrèges and Emmanuel Ungaro. Their bold, futuristic creations were constructed from plastic, paper, PVC, Lucite, leather and Perspex. Perspex was first used during the Second World War to make canopies for fighter planes; airmen would heat the material to create baubles to send to their girlfriends back

D&E STONE BRACELET
D&E, an American jewelry manufacturer, is known for its lavish use of large and colorful stones. Of special interest are the prong-set, domed, teardrop cabochons next to the large aurora borealis crystals.

KJL SHELL BROOCH
Kenneth Jay Lane, a
master of the unusual,
created this shell brooch
in the late 1960s. He
combined contrasting
materials—organic and
manufactured—in a hand-
soldered, black-plated
brass wire frame that
drapes over the top and
bottom of the shell to
support rhinestones in
various shapes and colors.

home. Now shoe and costume jewelry designers—influenced by modern artists such as Mondrian and Vasarely—made creations out of synthetic materials in saturated shades of pink, turquoise, orange and yellow or in stark black and white. Even Marcel Boucher, the master of real-looking jewelry, designed an Op Art collection in acid-colored enamels.

The new attitude to costume jewelry was that its value was not tied to the intrinsic worth of the materials. Skinny models wore miniskirts in magazine spreads, inspiring the young (and the not-so-young) to emulate mod styles by revealing the stomach, thighs and arms—all of which beckoned for adornment. Rudi Gernreich created the infamous topless bathing suit that could be accessorized with pectorals made up of metallic strands, although the majority of women kept their shirts on and wore oversize bracelets, rings and clips.

By the late sixties, however, women had tired of aggressive fabrics and unisex looks. Many young people had traveled to India (as the Beatles did) and had returned infatuated with Oriental fashions. Loose flowing caftans, djellabahs and vintage market finds in limp fabrics became the rage. Gilt chains, strings of glass beads, bangles, earrings and anklets with little bells were the accessories of choice. Trifari created the exotic Jewels of India collection in 1966 with opulent gems meant to look like jade, rubies and emeralds. Kenneth Jay Lane made dramatic, tongue-in-cheek, 5-inch paisley pins encrusted with multicolored stones. He also designed earrings out of peacock feathers, iridescent beetle bodies and embroidery—echoing the trust-fund-hippie trend in fashion made popular by It Girl Talitha Getty.

Both Schreiner and Helen Marion, the chief designer of Coro's high-end line Vendome, continued to use quality crystal rhinestones in their designs. Vendome produced a series of abstract fine-art collage pins inspired by Georges Braque, as well as a collection of opulent ethnic jewelry. At the same time, new designers were embracing the aesthetic possibilities of beads.

Thanks to the buzz created by the 1960 Olympics in Rome, and aided by the high cost of labor in France, Italy had become the new nucleus for high fashion in Europe. The brother-and-sister team of Coppola e Toppo showed a flair for meeting the needs of magazine fashion photography with dramatic bib collars made of colored plastic that looked like crystal stones. These mammoth woven collars had the affront of medieval armor about them, softened by the use of feminine, pastel-hued "stones." Coppola e Toppo's enormous chromatic and dimensional pieces were relatively inexpensive yet opulent and were highly favored by Valentino, Lancetti, Schon and Pucci. Their creations were also worn by Ava Gardner, Elizabeth Taylor and Jacqueline Kennedy.

Two lesser-known names deserve to be recognized here. Juliana was a label that was manufactured for only two years (1967–1968), creating fewer than two thousand pieces by chief designer William DeLizza. His distinctive style can be found in a series of Easter Egg collars and pins, as well as in parures of dazzling, high-color stones with chained-back construction. Rafael Alfandary was a well-respected Canadian

KJL BROOCH
Highly articulated and detailed figurals are among the most sought-after KJL pieces. This lion has a brushed-gold back, amber cabochon eyes that are bezel-set and a pavé-encrusted body of the finest rhinestones. The brooch is 3.5 inches long and is signed "KJL."

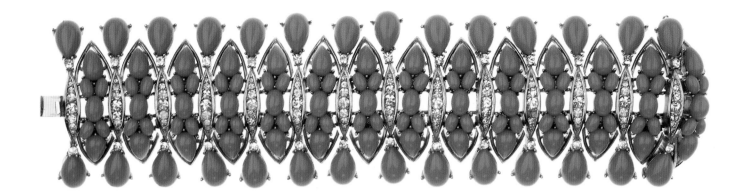

TRIFARI CUFF

Set in gold metal, with a frame surrounding
each link, this crossover piece alternates
dramatic pavé with large teardrop-shaped
turquoise cabochons. The bracelet is an
impressive 2 inches wide.

designer who produced his signature brass medallion necklaces and bracelets with large bezel-set center stones in the sixties and seventies. His bohemian braided chain jewels are still produced today.

Many people attribute the downfall of quality costume jewelry to the influx of cheap chain pieces in the early 1970s. By then, the fashion mantra was "Anything goes." Women wore mini, midi and maxi skirt lengths, jeans, ethnic designs, stretchy discowear and Diane von Furstenberg's iconic wrap dresses sans zipper, "Because," she said, "you're supposed to take them off without noise." Of all the eras so far, the seventies stands out as being the least focused on jewelry—epitomized in 1977, perhaps, when Bianca Jagger rode into Studio 54, in New York, on a white horse led by a naked man wearing nothing but metallic body paint.

Still, lightweight costume jewelry, particularly oversize plastic earrings, remained popular for dancing the night away in discos. In New York, a new fashion minimalism was on the horizon, promoted by designers Halston and Calvin Klein, who accessorized their dresses with only the most discreet Elsa Peretti jewels from Tiffany. In London, in the spring of 1977, the Queen celebrated her Silver Jubilee wearing a pink silk dress from Hardy Amies. However, down at her King's Road boutique, Sex, designer Vivienne Westwood was ripping up T-shirts and accessorizing them with punk "jewels"—safety pins, razor blades and metal spikes. The Summer of Love was officially over.

RAFAEL BRONZE PENDANT
Rafael's designs were popular in the 1970s. He was especially known for his large, bold, pendant necklaces in brass with single glass-stone accents. Rafael closed up shop in the 1980s, but he and his wife continued to design clocks and one-of-a-kind rings until Rafael's death in 2005.

Through the seventies, there was a movement from permissive hippiedom to a more minimal approach to fashion and accessories. Caught in the middle of the decade, these women are wearing divergent styles—a strong, iconic pendant and a strangely girlish dress. This dichotomy is typical of the seventies aesthetic.

TRIFARI'S ETERNAL APPEAL

Trifari started manufacturing costume jewelry in the 1930s and its delightful pieces are still in production today—a testament to the workmanship and timelessness of the designs.

JEWELS IN FLIGHT
Trifari produced two wonderful Wings series, one in the 1930s and a second in the 1960s. The animals and insects shown here were created in red enamel with crystal accents and flat, carved jade-like stones.

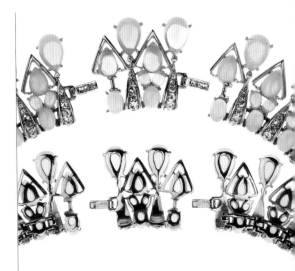

PINK CABOCHON NECKLACE

This rare Trifari masterpiece has teardrop and oval cabochon clusters set in gold prongs and casings alternating with diamanté wedges. Unique to the design is the invisible extension (*detail, above*), which allows the wearer to adjust the length of the necklace.

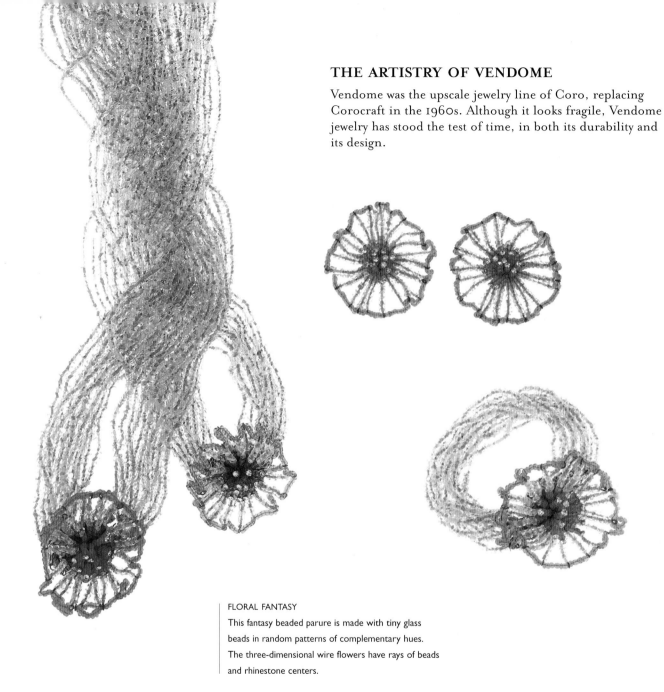

THE ARTISTRY OF VENDOME

Vendome was the upscale jewelry line of Coro, replacing
Corocraft in the 1960s. Although it looks fragile, Vendome
jewelry has stood the test of time, in both its durability and
its design.

FLORAL FANTASY

This fantasy beaded parure is made with tiny glass
beads in random patterns of complementary hues.
The three-dimensional wire flowers have rays of beads
and rhinestone centers.

BEAUTIFUL BOWS
This fanciful bow set illustrates the playful and creative style that was typical of Vendome designs. All have wire frames and faceted aurora borealis glass bugle beads. *(Left)* The large bow sports diamanté-studded, prong-set balls.

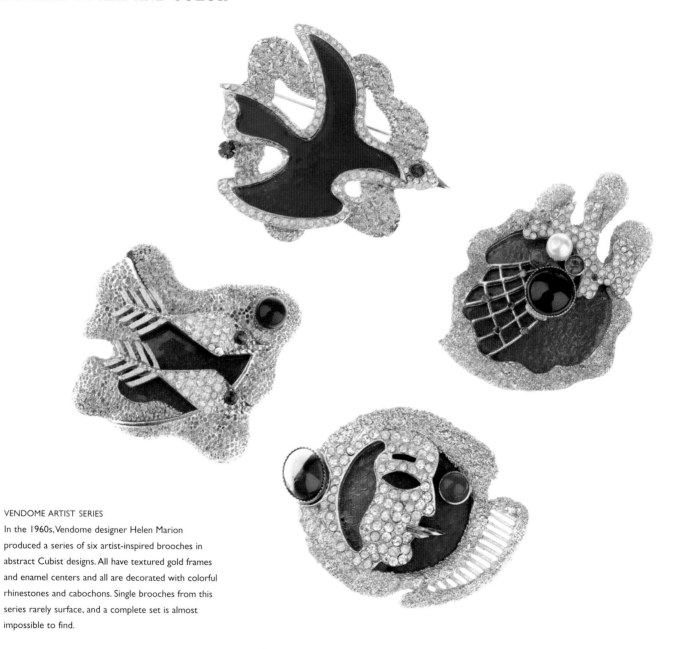

VENDOME ARTIST SERIES
In the 1960s, Vendome designer Helen Marion
produced a series of six artist-inspired brooches in
abstract Cubist designs. All have textured gold frames
and enamel centers and all are decorated with colorful
rhinestones and cabochons. Single brooches from this
series rarely surface, and a complete set is almost
impossible to find.

KJL BRACELETS AND BROOCH

These are perfect examples of KJL's extravagant design and use of color. *(Above)* Crossover hinge bracelets feature ferocious pavé animal heads and coral and turquoise cabochons. *(Below)* The 6.5-inch brooch is a bold fashion statement in a symphony of colors contained within a prong-set teardrop border.

D&E, JULIANA

William DeLizza and Harold Elster opened shop in 1947, with DeLizza in the role of chief designer. They produced lines of jewelry for more than eight hundred companies, including Coro, Garne, Kramer, and Weiss and Coventry.

There has been much controversy in the world of collecting about the attributions of Juliana designs. The consensus is that, along with its many other lines, D&E was the manufacturer of Juliana. The jewelry was hand-tagged for retail sale, rather than signed, and was produced for only two years in the late 1960s. The work that was known originally as Juliana is now referred to as D&E.

D&E designs are known for their liberal use of color, often in unusual combinations. Innovative constructions are also a trademark, the best known of which is the five-link roller band seen on most of the bracelets.

The height of D&E jewelry production was in the 1960s and 1970s. The factory closed in the late 1990s.

D&E BIB SET
This is a typical design from D&E, with a great variety of color in the center, tapering to a single row of crystals on each side. The large, oval stones are set in fancy prongs, and many are unfoiled.

D&E PARURE

This rare set is classic D&E style—clean lines with tight settings, plenty of color and unusual oval stones. It features three tiers of pronged, colored rhinestones adorned with cabochons in gold casings. The 2-inch bracelet is studded with prong-set, multicolored rhinestones.

D&E DAZZLE AND DRAMA

These highly collectible bracelets were produced in a
wide variety of colors and designs. *(Above)* The five-link
bracelet is the most recognizable as a D&E creation.
(Top) The open-back, 2-inch-wide bracelet has gold
Victorian-style casings around its colorful fancy stones.
(Far right) The open-back bracelet is studded with
gold filigree balls, peridots, pink prong-set navettes and
two gorgeous rivoli stones. *(Right)* Note the innovative
roller construction on the reverse side of a D&E bracelet.

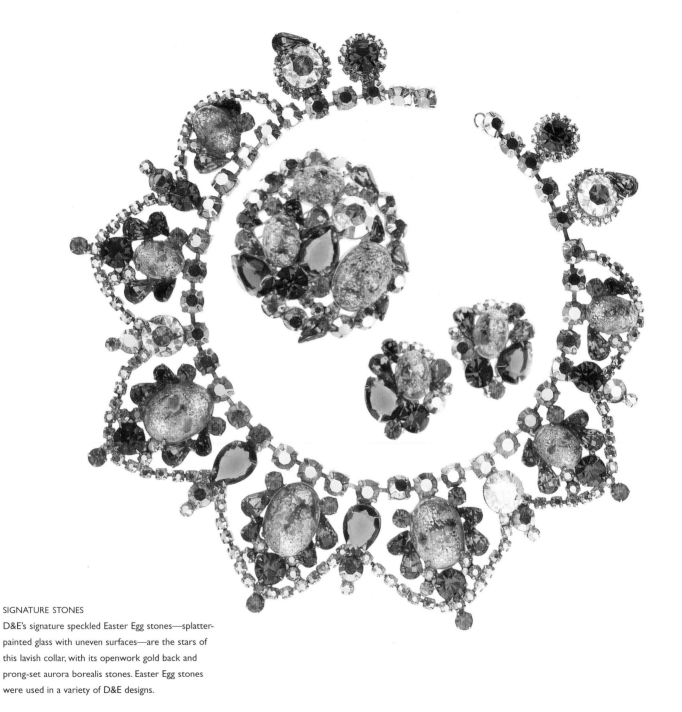

SIGNATURE STONES

D&E's signature speckled Easter Egg stones—splatter-painted glass with uneven surfaces—are the stars of this lavish collar, with its openwork gold back and prong-set aurora borealis stones. Easter Egg stones were used in a variety of D&E designs.

SOFT, SENSUOUS STATEMENTS IN GLASS

MAZER BRACELET AND BROOCHES
Carved glass leaves atop ornate paste caps star
in these pieces by Adolfo, who designed for Mazer
Brothers in the 1970s. The firm's creations, many
inspired by styles from the 1940s, were reasonably
priced for such high quality.

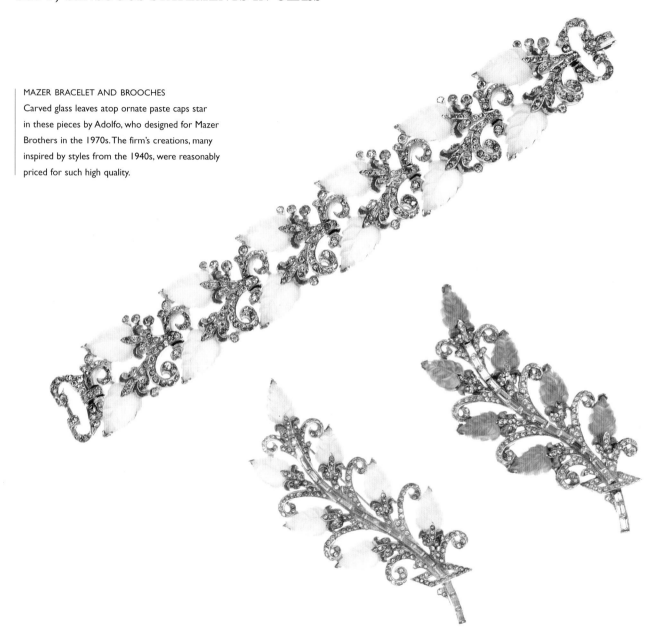

UNSIGNED NECKLACE AND BRACELET SET

Although one can never be certain of the provenance of unsigned pieces, the pink stones set in large, fancy prongs in this bracelet and necklace suggest Schreiner's workmanship and style.

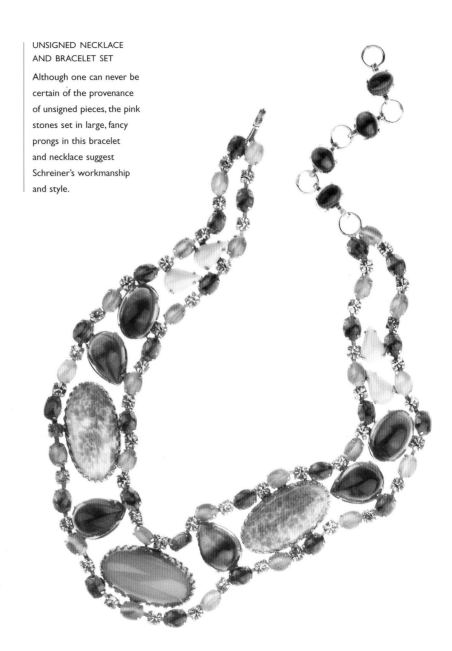

BOLD AND STYLISH KJL

The designs of Kenneth Jay Lane have always made a big splash. He is able to work in many different styles and takes inspiration from historical and artistic sources ranging from ancient Egypt to Art Deco. The most collectible of Kenneth Jay Lane's pieces are those produced up to the late 1970s. Jewelry from this period bears the coveted signature "KJL." Designs produced in the 1980s and beyond are signed either "Kenneth Jay Lane" or "Kenneth Lane" and are not yet as collectible as his earlier work.

HARLEQUIN NECKLACES
KJL created these striking necklaces in the late 1970s. They are made of trapezoidal and triangular jet and German glass, mounted in black-plated metal. The alternating positive-negative design creates simple but engaging works of art.

COPPOLA E TOPPO CREATIONS

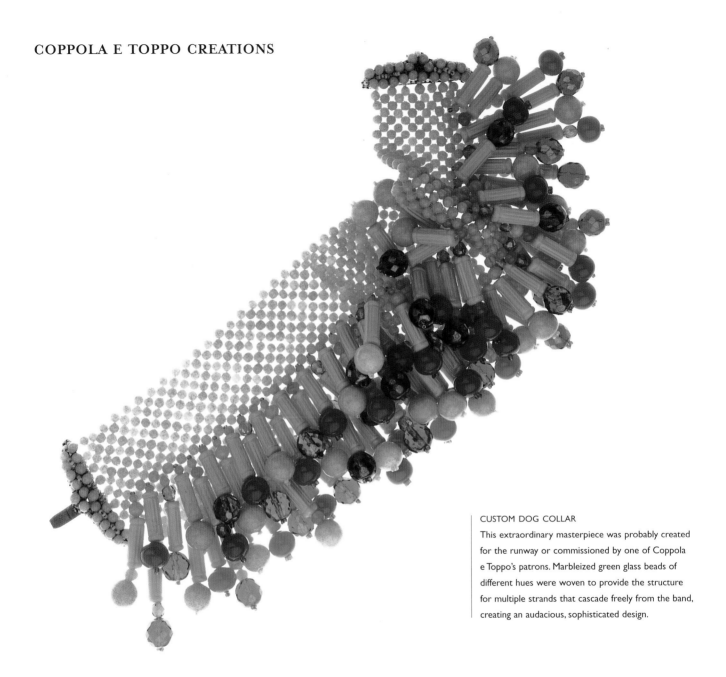

CUSTOM DOG COLLAR

This extraordinary masterpiece was probably created for the runway or commissioned by one of Coppola e Toppo's patrons. Marbleized green glass beads of different hues were woven to provide the structure for multiple strands that cascade freely from the band, creating an audacious, sophisticated design.

MULTISTRAND CRYSTAL NECKLACES
Classic Coppola e Toppo, these exquisitely made
necklaces of colored crystals end in a double-beaded
cluster clasp, which bears the designers' signature.

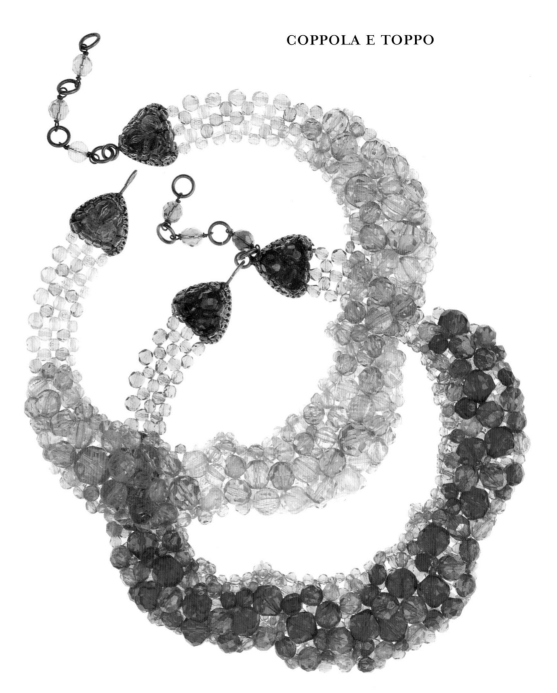

STRUCTURED NECKLACES
The beads of these
necklaces were tightly
woven, resulting in a rigid
form. Produced in small
quantities, they are very
difficult to find today.

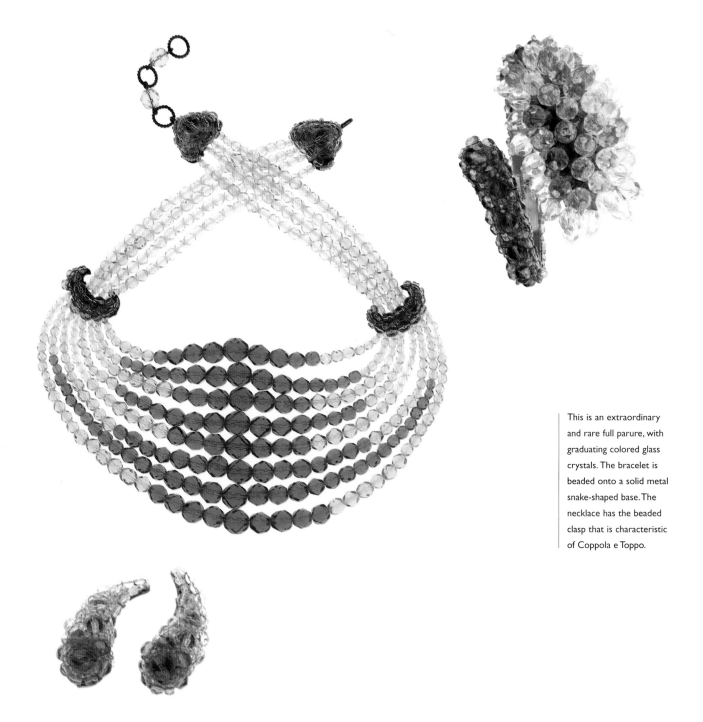

This is an extraordinary
and rare full parure, with
graduating colored glass
crystals. The bracelet is
beaded onto a solid metal
snake-shaped base. The
necklace has the beaded
clasp that is characteristic
of Coppola e Toppo.

UNSIGNED NECKLACE
Beautifully feminine, this flower garland is made of poured-glass clusters, beads with gold filigree crowns and unique oblong glass beads with painted designs. The intricacy is typical of high-quality French jewelry.

CHRISTIAN DIOR NECKLACE SET
This set, signed "Dior" and dated 1969, shows
some similarities to the unsigned necklace on the
opposite page. It, too, is of poured-glass clusters,
although it is a bolder, more formal design.

CHANEL BOW NECKLACE
Production of Chanel's fine jewelry line continued into the 1990s. This structured diamanté-encrusted collar is the revival of a 1932 design. It maintains its shape on and off the neck and shows the same quality of work-manship as the early version, with a slight variation in the design of the three-dimensional bow. It is signed "c Chanel 93."

The Eighties
& Nineties

(1980–1999)

GARISH, MINIMAL, SEVERE

EXPANSION BRACELET
This unique unsigned piece is in a green enamel petal design with crystal bezel-set teardrops. Some collectors attribute the bracelet to Chanel because of the boldness of its style and its beautiful workmanship.

As the millennium approached, fashion trends fragmented. Punk had burned out after only a few years and by the start of the eighties, ostentation was the order of the day. The hit television soap operas *Dallas* and *Dynasty* riveted viewers week after week with a fashion feast of big hair, power suits, silky dresses in bold colors and chunky gilt and paste jewelry. Years before, Jacqueline Kennedy Onassis had commissioned Kenneth Jay Lane to copy gems that Aristotle Onassis had given her. Now these baubles were being worn by the lead characters on the shows, prompting Jacqueline to tell Lane, "I saw our necklace on *Dynasty* the other day."

In England, Lady Diana Spencer—the lovely and exciting new addition to the royal family—dazzled the world with a fresh, sophisticated style that was instantly the fashion rage. Searching for other inspiration, designers plundered multiple eras for their collections. In the early eighties, Azzedine Alaia, Vivienne Westwood and Jean Paul Gaultier revisited Victorian corsetry that would become ubiquitous in the nineties. Meanwhile, Japanese designers—such as Rei Kawakubo for Commes des Garçons—were creating dark, voluminous, body-concealing clothes made from distressed, ragpicker fabrics.

Costume jewelry in the eighties was big and brash, a bold retort to the dress-for-success uniforms women were wearing—wide-shouldered jackets and skirts or pantsuits, high-heeled pumps with color-coordinated clutches or quilted Chanel-like handbags with gilt-metal chains. Eric Beamon created extravagant "kitchen sink" designs made from reconstituted fifties crystals, glass beads and ethnic jewelry. And Billy Boy, another American designer, who worked for Thierry Mugler, Hanae Mori and Diane von Furstenberg, made naïve, oversized brooches, necklaces and bangles from home-cooked resin and from glass stones.

Two other talents from this period are Larry Vrba and Robert Sorrell. Vrba worked as chief designer at Miriam Haskell during the seventies, then launched a solo career in the mid-eighties. Vrba draws his inspiration from vintage jewels, painstakingly handcrafting antique materials into large and ornate, yet gracious, styles. He is also known for his 4- and 5-inch Christmas tree pins. His creations are highly favored for costumes in artistic circles, including the Metropolitan Opera, Broadway productions and films.

Robert Sorrell is strongly influenced by fine jewelry of the forties and fifties. In addition to creating runway pieces for designers such as Thierry Mugler, Sorrell works on his own collections, drawing inspiration from Sotheby's and Doyle auction catalogs. Each of his jewels is handcrafted using the finest crystals and stones in impeccable settings. He is one of the first contemporary jewelers to make vintage-looking collections that fuse different design periods. For example, he will use a modern color

IRADJ MOINI BROOCH
No two pieces by Iranian designer Moini are alike. His large creations in brass, copper and crystals are all handmade. The designs, like this beetle brooch, are fanciful and have universal appeal.

scheme to "reinterpret" a classic thirties shape. Sorrell's creations are worn by performers in Cirque du Soleil and they are the adornment of choice at the annual Gay Pride parade in New York.

In 1985, Donna Karan launched her own label with a brilliant collection called Seven Easy Pieces. The all-black, tubular, wool jersey clothing was created for the modern career woman. To accessorize the stark pieces, Karan turned to jewelry designer Robert Lee Morris. The self-trained Morris hated decorative jewelry and rebeled against it by creating Amazonian-like appendages in 24-karat gold plate. "My view of what jewelry could mean had forever changed," said Karan of Morris's work. "I no longer thought of Robert's work as jewelry…[but as] art for the body."

During this period, Morris developed his signature alpha, beta and gamma cuffs, and these—as well as his sleek collars, rings and earrings—were frequently seen in fashion magazines. Morris had unwittingly developed a new jewelry category called "bridge" or "designer" jewelry. In price, it was somewhere between fine jewelry and costume, and retailers had a difficult time placing it in their stores.

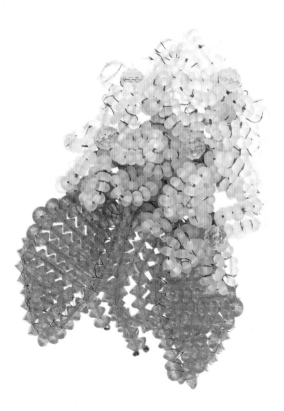

BEADED BROOCHES

(Top) Fashion designer Cristobal Balenciaga produced jewelry to complement each House of Balenciaga seasonal collection. The large blue dome brooch of graduating glass beads and diamanté rondelles is made as exquisitely as Balenciaga couture. *(Left)* Charming and fresh, the unsigned daisy brooch is made of clusters of white frosted beads with yellow faceted centers and bi-cone-shaped bead leaves.

Morris decided to open his own shop called Artwear, where he also acted as curator selling the works of other talented designers. The boutique was popular with such fashion cognoscenti as Marella Agnelli, Liza Minnelli, Andy Warhol and Bianca Jagger.

Alongside the new minimalism touted by Calvin Klein, Donna Karan and a host of Japanese and Belgian designers, the French and the Italians maintained their devotion to conventional notions of luxury. During the eighties, many design houses were making their own lines of jewelry, produced in limited quantities—and these are, I believe, tomorrow's collectibles. In 1983, Karl Lagerfeld took the helm of Chanel and reinvigorated the brand with his irreverent and lavish use of the double-C logo in costume jewels and handbags. Lagerfeld also created whimsical couture gems tied to each season's fashion theme. For example, his Monte Carlo Ballet collection was accessorized with furniture and chandeliers modeled on those in his own château; his French Patisserie collection contained witty jewels shaped like éclairs, petits fours and croissants.

In 1987, Christian Lacroix introduced the "puff dress," which caught on like wildfire. Lacroix, the quintessentially Parisian designer, brought fashion and jewelry closer together (much the way Schiaparelli did in the forties and fifties) by creating gowns and jackets embellished with heavy embroidery, sequins and jewelry. He also produced a range of costume jewels for each of his fashion lines: couture, prêt-à-porter and diffusion. Classic Lacroix motifs are hearts, his initials, massive folkloric pendants, cuffs and belts in shocking color combinations of red and pink or purple and orange. Many of these pieces are molded by hand and painted in gold.

MIMI SHULMAN BROOCH
This antique ribbon-medal brooch was a complement to the military-inspired fashions of the late 1980s. To soften it, Canadian designer Shulman added a three-dimensional silk rose, silver filigree top and her signature dangling charms.

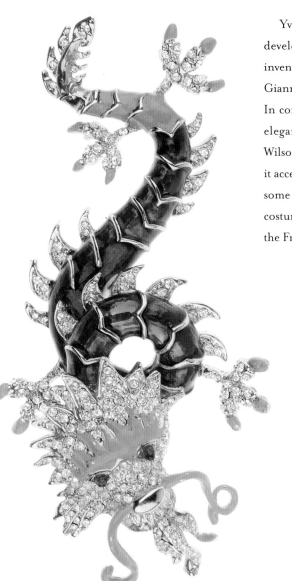

Yves Saint Laurent worked closely with muse Loulou de la Falaise, who developed his signature larger-than-life cuffs using new resin formulas invented by the manufacturers Goossens, and Migeon and Migeon. In Italy, Gianni Versace's collections epitomized the glitz and excess of the eighties. In contrast, Giorgio Armani accessorized his tailored clothes with typically elegant yet bold costume jewels—such as the dragonfly pin by Butler & Wilson, the highly respected British design team who single-handedly made it acceptable to wear diamanté during the day in the United Kingdom! With some notable exceptions, American and British fashion designers treated costume jewelry as an afterthought to their runway presentations, whereas the French and the Italians integrated costume pieces into their collections.

DRAGON BROOCH AND LACROIX EARRINGS
This Butler & Wilson dragon brooch, of metallic enamel and pavé-set rhinestones, and the pearl dangle earrings by Christian Lacroix are fine examples of the strident style typical of costume jewelry in the 1980s and early 1990s.

By the late 1980s, the prescient designers Geoffrey Beene, in New York, and Yohji Yamamoto, in Tokyo, were predicting a backlash against overdressing and ostentatious accessories. Diana Vreeland passed away in 1989, marking the end of the era of fashion giddiness. By the early nineties, the demise of the Soviet Union, wars in Europe and the Middle East, the AIDS crisis, cyberculture, and political and corporate corruption all contributed to a somber and anxious mood. As if in penance for the excesses of the previous decade, people wore blank black clothes with only large Gothic crosses as adornments. Heroin chic and grunge were the fashion buzzwords. Runway shows became fin-de-siècle spectacles. Dolce & Gabbana showed gangster motifs; Alexander McQueen referred to rapes and genocide.

Couture fashion jewelry reflected our changing relationship to body, space and time. Models in Hussein Chalayan's Spring/Summer 1996 collection sported mouth jewels such as the silver "mouth bar," which was inserted vertically behind the front teeth to keep the mouth open. Alexander McQueen's Fall/Winter 1996 collection showed models with silver rose thorns stuck to their faces, and thorn necklaces and bracelets resembling barbed wire.

The world did not end on New Year's Eve 1999, but the gloomy fashions *did* make people too depressed to shop. Frantic retailers would ensure that by the dawn of the new millennium, "retail therapy" would be alive and well.

LUCITE CUFF
At once contemporary and vintage-looking, this unusual bracelet of Lucite surrounding large faceted stones and pavé diamanté accents harks back to 1930s designs in Lucite and Apple Juice Bakelite. The gold frame is hinged.

COOL AND GRAPHIC ICE-CUBE JEWELS

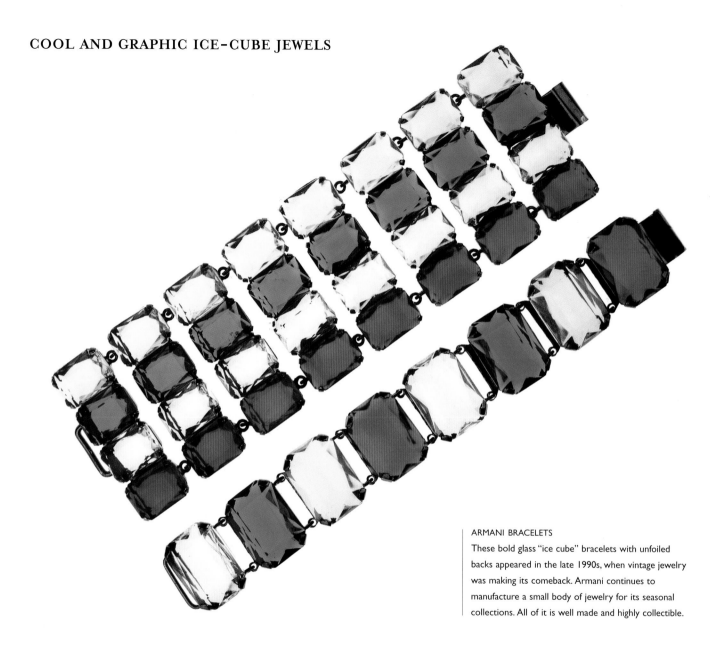

ARMANI BRACELETS
These bold glass "ice cube" bracelets with unfoiled backs appeared in the late 1990s, when vintage jewelry was making its comeback. Armani continues to manufacture a small body of jewelry for its seasonal collections. All of it is well made and highly collectible.

ACRYLIC ICE
Playful and creative, this unsigned necklace is a wonderful example of the popular acrylic jewelry of the 1980s and 1990s. Alternating black and clear cubes dangle in clusters, while thin silver and transparent disks provide extra interest.

MAISON GRIPOIX

FLORAL PÂTE DE VERRE

Madame Gripoix designed for Chanel, Worth and
Dior from the 1920s through the 1940s. In the
1990s, Maison Gripoix was known for its pâte
de verre, or poured-glass, line called Histoire de
Verre. This poured-glass openwork necklace
is gloriously light and alive, with its flowers of
different hues and sizes. The glass is set in
gilt-wire rope frames.

A DREAM OF A NECKLACE

ARTISANAL NECKLACE
This brass moon-and-star necklace is one of many beautiful pieces of costume jewelry created by artisans in the late 1990s.

HASKELL IN THE NINETIES

Haskell continued to produce fabulous jewels into the nineties, and the commitment to excellence in workmanship and design didn't waver at any point in the company's history.

PEARL LOZENGE
NECKLACE AND EARRINGS

This triple-strand Baroque pearl necklace, with its elaborate center dangle of filigree-backed pendants and gold-crowned pearls, is a dazzling example of the ongoing quality of Haskell designs through the decades.

HASKELL DEMI-PARURE
This fringe necklace is made of graduated colored and clear bi-cone-shaped glass beads on a gold cable chain. The set was a special-order item in the early 1990s and only two such necklaces were ever made. The clasp is signed.

MARGOT DE TAXCO AND LUCY BERGAMINI

Originally a watercolor artist, Margot de Taxco began
designing jewelry in the 1930s. Her designs encompass
diverse styles ranging from traditional Mexican silver
to Art Deco enamel. De Taxco jewelry in animal motifs
is particularly collectible. American artisanal jeweler
Lucy Bergamini is wildly experimental with handmade
glass beads.

DE TAXCO SNAKE PARURE

A later rendition of de Taxco's articulated snake
set of the 1940s, this gorgeous version is slightly
larger in scale than the original. Both necklace and
bracelet have articulated links of speckled enamel
with silver detailing and blue stones. The set is
signed "925, TF-32 Mexico."

LUCY BERGAMINI NECKLACE
This glass-and-sterling-silver charm design is whimsical, creative and fresh. Unique glass-encased beads create a rainbow of interest and detail.

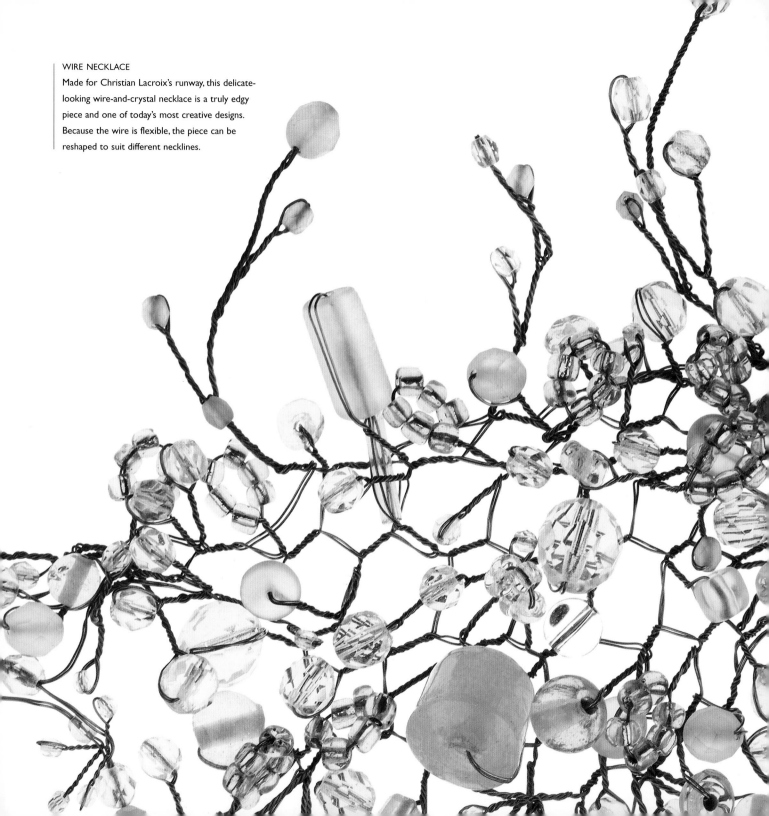

WIRE NECKLACE
Made for Christian Lacroix's runway, this delicate-
looking wire-and-crystal necklace is a truly edgy
piece and one of today's most creative designs.
Because the wire is flexible, the piece can be
reshaped to suit different necklines.

Into the Twenty-First Century

(2000–PRESENT)

A RETURN TO FABULOUS

ACETATE BROOCH
This acetate blossom is a nineties revival of the popular acetate flowers of the sixties. The leaves are actually repurposed from vintage floral centerpieces.

The nineties saw the rise of the mediocre in fashion and design. Whether it was clothing from Gap and Banana Republic or home decor from Martha Stewart, "correct taste"—at a modest price—was what everyone wanted. In this sea of banality, fashion mavens started to reacquaint themselves with the whimsy and the beauty of vintage clothing and jewelry. On the red carpets, Hollywood starlets dazzled in vintage gowns from Madame Grès, Valentino and Lanvin—accessorizing these beautiful creations with antique gems from Fred Leighton or Neil Lane. Miuccia Prada, named one of the World's 100 Most Influential People by *Time* magazine, flipped Coco Chanel's jewelry style upside down. Chanel wore her faux gems with the hauteur that one associates with real gems. Prada, on the other hand, accessorized her sweater-and-skirt ensembles with fine antique diamond necklaces and tiaras, with the casualness usually associated with wearing costume jewels.

The early years of the new millennium saw an explosion of interest in embellishment that can be viewed as a consensual thumbing of the nose at the minimalism and doom-and-gloom of the nineties. In the previous decade, perhaps in response to the recession, a growing awareness of the AIDS crisis and global wars, consumers had wanted to buy the real thing. Moderately priced jewelry from Stephen Dweck, Robert Lee Morris, John Hardy, Ralph Lauren and David Yurman—made with silver, gold plate and semiprecious stones—proved popular. Today, in a more economically robust era, jewelry in both real and faux materials is worn to give ensembles a personal, sophisticated, yet nostalgic look. Just as no single designer dictates fashion trends, no single piece of jewelry style suits every occasion. Women mix and match jewelry to suit their moods. Necklaces that at one time would not be worn together are now grouped in a casual fashion. Bracelets that have no obvious color or textural format are arbitrarily stacked up the arm.

Although there are many talented fashion and jewelry designers, the industry today is so trend-driven and narrowly focused on shareholder profits that styles do not last beyond a season or two. When one thinks of the collections by Schiaparelli, Chanel and Yves Saint Laurent, so richly informed by the arts, travel, philosophy and great books, it is little wonder that their couture jewels are still among the most collectible and wearable treasures today.

In the forties, fifties and sixties, costume jewelry houses such as Trifari, Eisenberg Originals and Napier had their own distinctive styles and advertised heavily in fashion magazines. Today, except for Swarovski and Swatch, ads for faux designs have been replaced by campaigns from fine jewelry houses, such as Cartier, Bulgari and Harry Winston, and from fashion houses. Of course, high-end costume jewels continue to be produced by Dior, YSL, Prada, Valentino, Armani, Miu Miu, Marni, Helmut Lang, Jean Paul Gaultier, Lanvin and Chanel, and are sold in their own boutiques worldwide.

ROBERT SORRELL BRACELET
American designer Sorrell draws his inspiration from the best jewelry of the forties and fifties. His extravagant, theatrical pieces use the finest rhinestones and Swarovski crystals and are always impeccably set. The oval crystals and the round rhinestones on this cuff embrace a huge purple cabochon.

BOLD AND BEAUTIFUL—COSTUME JEWELRY TODAY

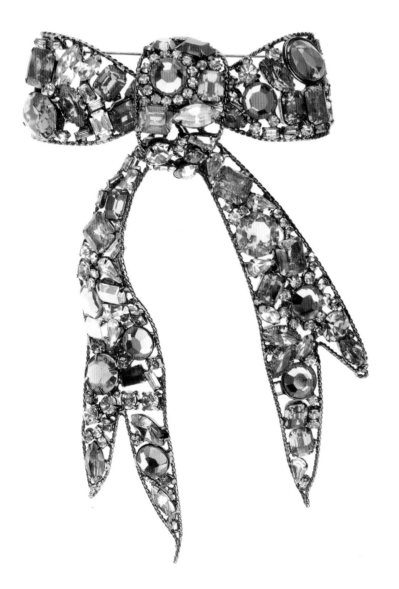

VRBA BOW AND CHRISTMAS TREE BROOCHES
These unique knotted bow and Christmas tree designs are signature motifs for Larry Vrba, who worked for Haskell, Castlecliff and DeLillo before launching his own line of spectacular pieces in the early 1980s. The dramatic impact of Vrba's designs has made him a favorite of costume designers and anyone with a love of the theatrical.

SORRELL NECKLACE
The intricacy and detail of this bib necklace are extraordinary. Sorrell's use of the best crystals makes its pieces comparable to precious jewelry, though they are larger and splashier. Here, prong-set clear crystals and baguettes are the backdrop for brilliant, tear-shaped jade glass dangles. Sorrell designs are widely respected by collectors and are signed "Sorrell Original."

ELMA BEADED NECKLACES

An Italian designer who is fascinated by glass beads,
Elma works her designs to reflect the beads'
inherent aesthetic appeal. The multicolored smoke
crystal necklace has a triple flower clasp of woven
beads, and matching flower earrings. It and the
deep red crystal-beaded collar show similarities
to the 1960s creations of Coppola e Toppo.

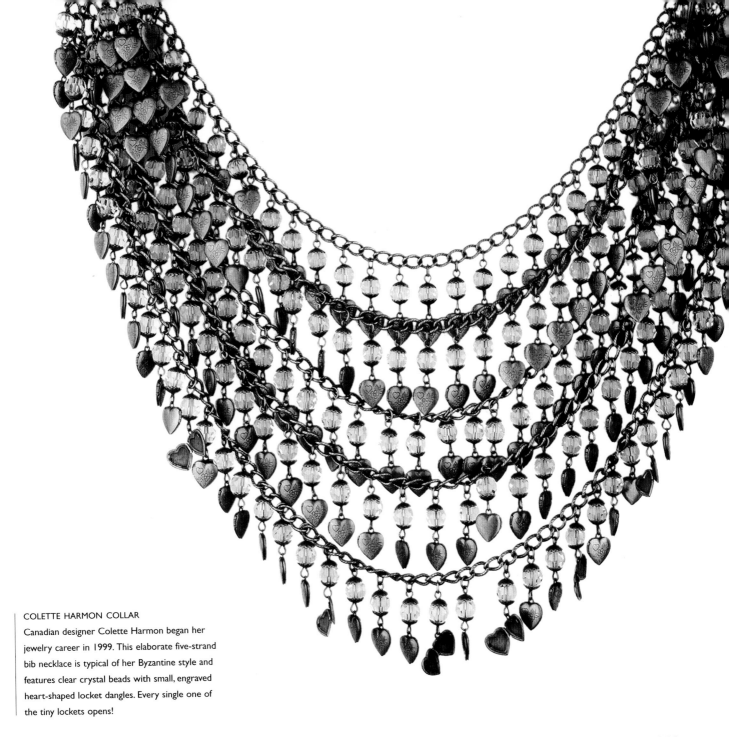

COLETTE HARMON COLLAR

Canadian designer Colette Harmon began her jewelry career in 1999. This elaborate five-strand bib necklace is typical of her Byzantine style and features clear crystal beads with small, engraved heart-shaped locket dangles. Every single one of the tiny lockets opens!

COLLECTING VINTAGE COSTUME JEWELRY

The current general interest in vintage jewelry—both for personal use and as a valuable collectible—is robust, thus making good pieces scarce. Museums, such as the Victoria & Albert in London, the Metropolitan Museum in New York and the Royal Ontario Museum in Toronto, have begun to develop strong collections of vintage jewels. Fine auction houses such as Sotheby's and Doyle regularly put costume pieces up for auction, with prices competing with those for fine gemstones. Many reproductions of key designs—Jelly Bellies, Haskells and Eisenberg Originals—abound. As with any significant investment, the rule is caveat emptor. Here are some suggestions to help you make wise purchases of vintage costume jewelry.

• Make sure the dealer is reputable and knowledgeable.

• Step back and appraise the design. Is it original, pleasing to the eye…?

• Notice the quality of the craftsmanship. Does it look like a sound, stable construction or is it flimsy? Are the stones set properly? Are the stones hand-set in prongs or glued in? Stones that are glued in can yellow or loosen over time.

• Take time to study the piece and ensure that it is in good condition. Ask the dealer if any repairs have been made. Look for evidence of soldering or cracks.

• Check the stones. Are they original? Also, notice if the stones have darkened or become cloudy. Are all the stones present?

• Check the clasp. Is it original? Check that clasps are intact and close properly.

- Ascertain whether the piece is a reproduction or an original. Unfortunately, many reproductions are priced as high as the originals, so do not use cost as your only guide.

- Ensure that the plating is in good condition. Look out for metal pitting, corrosion, thin plating, oxidation or worn enamel.

- Some Bakelite can be tested with Simichrome, a commercial product. Use a cotton-tipped swab to rub the Simichrome onto the Bakelite. The cotton should turn yellow if the jewelry is true Bakelite. Unfortunately, this test is not a guarantee, as some colors, such as black, will not show this effect.

- With Bakelite, look specifically for chips, fading, loose hinges and reproductions. Resin is not Bakelite and should not be represented as such. Some designers are repurposing Bakelite in new designs. This is legitimate but must be disclosed.

- Sometimes a piece can be flawed but still worthy of purchase. If I find a gem that is cracked or discolored but I adore it and it is not intended for resale, I will purchase it happily.

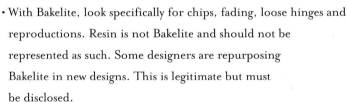

ACETATE FLOWER BROOCH
What's old is new again. Leaves from a 1960s centerpiece are now part of a vibrant 6-inch contemporary brooch.

GLOSSARY

AMAZONITE A semiprecious stone, ranging in color from dark green to blue-green.

AMBER The fossilized resin of conifers. Amber is often used in engraved jewelry.

AQUAMARINE A semiprecious gemstone in shades of blue and green.

ARTICULATED Jewelry with flexible joints or segments.

AURORA BOREALIS Crystals with a highly iridescent finish, created by Swarovski for Christian Dior. Named after the Northern Lights.

BAGUETTE A narrow, rectangular-cut rhinestone.

BAKELITE A moldable plastic invented by Leo Baekland in 1908. It was much used in costume jewelry from the twenties to the forties. Bakelite can be lathe-carved, and one color can be inlaid into another, as in polka dots.

BAROQUE PEARL An irregularly shaped pearl. Baroque pearls can be natural or artificial.

BEAD Any small object with a central, pierced hole that allows it to be strung.

BEZEL SETTING A setting that circles the entire stone with flanges soldered and folded over, or burnished over the edge.

BIB NECKLACE A necklace with pendants or chains arrayed to resemble a bib.

BOG OAK A dark brown fossilized material that came from Irish peat bogs and was used as a substitute for jet. It was particularly popular in the 1850s and was usually carved into shamrocks, castles and other Celtic motifs.

"C" CLASP The most common means of securing a brooch before 1900 or so, when safety catches were invented. The pin connected to one side of the brooch is threaded through a layer of the garment and rests in a C-shaped catch on the other side of the brooch. Since the C had no mechanism to hold the pin in place, pins were usually designed to be long enough to extend beyond the end of the brooch to weave back into the garment for security.

CABOCHON A smooth, unfaceted, dome-shaped stone with a flat back, or a paste stone with a flat back.

CELLULOID An early, highly flammable plastic (cellulose nitrate) introduced in 1869. It was used in costume jewelry and hair accessories until the 1920s. Used to imitate ivory, bone, tortoiseshell, coral and pearls.

CHANNEL SETTING Setting in which stones are held in place in a metal channel with a slight rim around the edges.

CHATELAINE Formerly used to describe a chain attached to an ornamental brooch or hook worn at the waist, from which were suspended various objects, such as keys, a watch, a purse or grooming items. Later used to describe pins connected by a chain.

CHATON CUT A smooth, central top surrounded by eight facets. Best used with smaller stones.

CLUSTER SETTING A setting in which small stones or pearls are set around a larger stone.

CROSSOVERS Costume jewelry that looks like it was made with precious stones. Boucher was one of the masters of crossovers.

CRYSTAL Highest quality, very clear glass that contains at least 10 percent lead oxide and looks like natural or rock crystal.

CUFF BRACELET A rigid, wide bracelet with a hinge and clasp.

CUSHION CUT A soft, rounded edge, rather than the hard, angular facets seen in most traditional stonecuts.

DEMI-PARURE A matching set of jewelry, consisting of two or three pieces.

DENTELLE Precursor of rhinestones, dentelle-shaped stones are cut in thirty-two or sixty-four facets for brilliance.

DIAMANTÉ Crystal or glass stones with many facets, cut to resemble gemstones. See *Rhinestones*.

DUETTE A brooch that can be worn as two separate pins or clipped together as one.

EMBOSSED Surface decoration in which a design is raised slightly above the surface.

EMERALD CUT A rectangular, faceted cut, also known as a "step" or "trap" cut.

ENAMEL A glassy material that is fused to metal, porcelain or other surfaces. Enameling reached a height of artistry in the forties and was revived in the sixties.

ENGRAVING A method of decorating a surface by etching it with a sharp tool.

FACET A small, flat surface cut into a stone or glass. Facets refract the light in order to enhance the brilliance of the stone.

FESTOON Also known as a garland. A short necklace with dangling ornaments.

FILIGREE Gold or silver wire that has been twisted into lacy patterns and soldered into place. Imitation filigree is made of stamped metal.

FOIL BACK A reflective metal coating or foil placed behind a gem or paste to enhance its color and light reflection.

FRENCH JET Shiny cut black glass designed to imitate real jet. Well suited to carving because it was less brittle than Whitby jet.

FRUIT SALAD Costume jewelry set with red, green and blue glass or plastic.

GALALITH Artificial horn made with plastic.

INVISIBLE SETTING Technique in which stones are fastened from the back, so it appears that there is no metal mount.

JAPANNING A process that colors metal a dull black. Originally used for mourning jewelry; later used to blacken a setting for decorative purposes.

JELLY BELLY An animal pin with a clear Lucite or glass stone as the "belly."

JET Fine-grained, petrified wood. Black and opaque, it has a velvety surface and was a popular material for mourning jewelry during the nineteenth century. Most jet is from Whitby, England. "Jet" may now refer to any black stone used in jewelry.

LUCITE A clear plastic that was patented by DuPont in 1937, Lucite is an acrylic resin.

MARCASITE Iron pyrites cut to look like diamonds, marcasite was used extensively in the costume jewelry of the twenties and thirties. Marcasite is often confused with cut steel.

GLOSSARY

MARQUISE CUT Faceted, elongated stone, pointed at both ends. See *Navette cut.*

MILLEFIORI A glassmaking technique in which lengths of different-colored glass are fused in bundles. The cross-section creates a pattern that looks like "a thousand flowers" (*millefiori*, in Italian). Millefiori glass can also be made into beads.

NAVETTE CUT An oval-shaped gemstone with points at both ends. See *Marquise cut.*

OPERA-LENGTH A very long necklace, extending anywhere from 48 inches to 120 inches.

PARURE A matching set of four or five pieces of jewelry, most often consisting of a necklace, earrings, a brooch or pin and at least one bracelet. See also *Demi-parure.*

PASTE Glass with a high lead content, which has been cut and faceted to look like a gemstone. Also known as diamanté or rhinestone.

PÂTE DE VERRE (Also known as poured glass). Crushed glass that has been colored with metal oxides, then fused, molded and fired. The result is an opaque, dense glass.

PAVÉ SETTING Setting in which stones are set so close together (*pavé* is the French word for "paved") that the backing is not visible, giving the effect of a continuous surface of jewels.

PEAR CUT Stone in the shape of a pear or teardrop; rounded at one end and pointed at the other.

PENDALOQUE Pendants and earrings in drop forms. Also used to refer to a precious stone that has been faceted in a pear or drop shape.

PLIQUE-À-JOUR Translucent enamel with no backing in a wire framework. The effect is reminiscent of stained glass.

POT METAL A base metal, made from an alloy of tin and lead, that was widely used in early-twentieth-century costume jewelry.

PRONG SETTING A setting in which stones are held in position by claw-like metal fingers.

RETRO JEWELRY A bold style of jewelry popular in the late thirties and forties, influenced by Art Deco Machine-Age forms. Retro costume jewelry was often made of vermeil in geometric shapes.

RHINESTONES Highly reflective crystal or glass stones cut to resemble gemstones. The original rhinestones were quartz stones from the Rhine River. See *Diamanté*.

RHODIUM A gray metal in the platinum family that is sometimes mistaken for silver. It is used for plating in costume jewelry because it is unusually hard and resistant to rust.

RONDELLES Small, round, jeweled beads often used as spacers between beads in necklaces or bracelets.

ROSE MONTÉE A faceted, flat-backed rhinestone, often mounted in a pierced metal cup, so that is can be wired onto clothes or jewelry. Rose montée was frequently used in embroidery for haute couture clothes.

SAUTOIR A long necklace popular in the twenties. Usually made of chains, beads or pearls and ending in a tassel or fringe.

SEED PEARLS Small round pearls, either natural or artificial.

SETTING The method of securing a stone in a piece of jewelry. Some settings are closed, which means that there is metal behind the stone. Open settings have no metal behind the stone, which allows light to shine through.

SOLDERING The practice of using solder, which has a low melting point, to join metals.

TREMBLER Jewelry with parts set on springs so that they tremble whenever the wearer of the jewelry moves.

VERMEIL Sterling silver plated with gold. Also called silver gilt or gold wash. During the forties, vermeil sterling silver was the material of choice for most American costume jewelers.

VULCANITE A hard, moldable dark brown or black plastic used for memorial pieces in the mid-Victorian period.

ACKNOWLEDGMENTS

Colleagues and friends have been asking me for years to publish a book on my personal collection of vintage costume jewelry. But it was not until my dear friend Sherry Heitler convinced me of the importance of sharing what I know and showing some of the unique treasures I have collected that I began to understand the true value that *Fabulous Fakes* would have to all jewelry lovers.

My friend Art Niemi, graphic designer extraordinaire, designed a mock-up of the book that attracted the attention of Madison Press Books, an international book producer that came highly recommended to me by my agent, Beverley Slopen. Brian Soye, Madison's president, and editors Wanda Nowakowska and Alison Maclean eased me through the creative process with their excellent communication, flexibility and psychological savvy. I could not have done this book without them.

Talented designer Gorette Costa, of Costa Leclerc Design, and superb photographer Puzant Apkarian really brought the collection to life. Rita Silvan, editor-in-chief of *ELLE* Canada, contributed wonderful essays on the historical context of costume jewelry. Bao-Nghi Nhan scoured the archives for historical images to complement the text. Robin Goldberg, Chris Curreri, Rebecca Oksner, Jill Ditner, Johanna Warwick and Suzanne Goldberg, from my office, worked tirelessly and graciously to get the facts right.

My New York publisher, Ann Bramson of Artisan, had a clear vision and an uncompromising demand for excellence. Ann was definitely a creative partner in the production of *Fabulous Fakes*.

When I first started collecting in the early eighties, I was fortunate to meet some wonderful people who helped shape my collection. Talya Dunleavy, Carol Moskowitz, Bill Brethour and Richard Fulton all affected my aesthetic judgment by introducing me to rare and beautiful examples of vintage costume jewelry. Later on in my collecting, I met Kendra Simmons, Conrad Vout, Cindy Calder, Dorothy Loud and Donna Frankel, all of whom understood my point of view and helped me to find treasures.

In 1995, I met Joel Rath, then president of Holt Renfrew Canada. He and Pat Di Bratto, vice president of the accessories division, were true visionaries who decided to create the Carole Tanenbaum Vintage Collection at their flagship store in Toronto, Canada. Mary Hinrichs, my most valued jewel, runs the department with knowledge and enthusiasm.

My New York jewelry agent, Ellen Carey, is my own personal rainmaker. She supported vintage jewelry before it was fashionable. I have the greatest admiration and respect for her prescience and for her professionalism.

Two men in my life have greatly influenced me. First, my father, Max Granick, who instilled in me a sense of aesthetics. His taste and critical acumen were well respected in the New York art world during his lifetime. Secondly, my husband, Howard. He has always encouraged me to follow my dreams. His guidance and wisdom have been his greatest gift to me.

— Carole Tanenbaum

PHOTOGRAPHY CREDITS

Puzant Apkarian photographed all the vintage costume jewelry featured in *Fabulous Fakes* except for the images in Chapter One, which were photographed by Luis Albuquerque. The following are the credits and sources for additional images included in the book:

11: (bottom) Roger Fenton / Getty Images.

39: (bottom) General Photographic Agency / Getty Images.

42: Topical Press Agency / Getty Images.

66: (left) Author's private collection.

107: Author's private collection.

167: (right) Evening Standard / Getty Images.

212: Stephane Cardinale / People Avenue / CORBIS.

INDEX

References to images and captions are indicated by italicized page numbers.

A

Adolpho, *178*
Adrian, Gilbert, 65
agate, 13, *32, 34–35*
Alaia, Azzedine, 190
Albert, Prince, 10, *11*, 12, 13, 14
Alfandary, Rafael, 166, *167*
Amourelle, 107, 116
Apple Juice Bakelite, 60, 66, 76
Armani, Giorgio, 194, *196*, 207
Art Deco and prewar period
       (1920–1935), 36–61
   Art Deco, *38–39*, 46, 50, 64
   Bakelite, 41, *44–45, 50–51*, 60, 61
   bangle, *60*
   bracelets, *44*, 46, 50, *52–53,
       56–57*
   brooches, *40–41*, 43–44, 46, *48–49,
       58–60*
   clips, *48*, 51
   earrings, *51*
   figurals, *45, 49*
   motifs, 41
   necklaces, *36, 38*, 40, *45, 47, 50–51,
       54–55*
Art Nouveau, 14, *24*, 29, 39, 46, 50
Arts and Crafts, 14, 46
aurora borealis, 106, 109
Austro-Hungarian style, *21*

B

Bakelite, 41, 61, 66, 67, 213
   Apple Juice, 60, 66, 76
   bangles, 66, *91*
   bracelets, *44*, 50, *75, 91*
   brooches, *44–45*, 60, 70, *73–75, 77, 88*
   carved, *76–77*
   earrings, *75*
   figurals, *45, 88*

necklaces, *38, 45, 50–51*, 76
   patriotic jewelry, 66, 70
Baker, Josephine, 40
Balenciaga, Cristobal, *192*
bangles, 60, 61, 66, *91*
Banton, Travis, 65
Beamon, Eric, 190
Beene, Geoffrey, 195
Bergamini, Lucy, *202, 203*
Billy Boy, 190
Birmingham, England, 10, 26
bloodstone, *32, 34, 35*
bog oak, 22
Bohemian jewelry, 13, 16
Bonaz, Auguste, *36*, 41
Boucher, Marcel, 41, 68, 79, 106,
       134–35, 164
bracelets
   agate, *35*
   angel, *12*
   Armani, *196*
   Art Deco and prewar, *44*, 46, 50,
       52–53, 56–57
   Bakelite, *44*, 50, *75, 91*
   bangles, 60, 61, 66, *91*
   Caviness, Alice, *144*
   Chanel, *190*
   cuffs, 194, *195*
   D&E, *163, 175–76*
   de Taxco, Margot, *202*
   DRGM, *50*
   Eighties & Nineties, *190, 195–197, 202*
   Fahrner, Theodor, *46*
   Fifties, *106, 108–109, 113, 117, 120,
       124, 126–32, 136–39, 141–44, 149*
   floral, *100*
   garnet, *13*
   Har, *136*
   Haskell, Miriam, *100, 106, 113*
   Hobé, William, *87–88*
   Hollycraft, *109*
   Jomaz, *137*

Jonné, *117*
Lane, Kenneth Jay, *173*
Ledo and Pierre, *139*
malachite, *33*
Mazer Brothers, *137, 178*
paste, *21*
portrait, *22*
post-Depression and war years, 69,
       75, *87–88, 90–91, 100*
   Retro style, 69
Robert Originals, *108*
Schiaparelli, *126–131*
Schreiner, Henry, *120, 124, 179*
Selro, *138*
Sherman, *132*
silver, *26*
Sixties & Seventies, *163, 166, 170,
       173, 175–76, 178–79*
Sorrell, Robert, 207
tortoiseshell, *12*
Trifari, *90–91, 166*
Vendome, *170*
Victorian era, *17–18, 26, 33, 35*
Victorian revival, *141*
Braendle, Gustav, 46
Braque, Georges, 165
brooches
   agate, *32*
   Amourelle, *116*
   Art Deco and prewar period, *40–41,
       43–44, 46, 48–49, 58–60*
   Bakelite, *44–45*, 60, 70, *73–75, 77, 88*
   Balenciaga, Cristobal, *192*
   birds, *21, 29, 41, 49, 71–72, 78, 79, 89,
       94, 99, 104, 133*
   bog oak, *22*
   Boucher, Marcel, *68*
   bows, *21, 65, 83, 84, 93, 98, 171, 208*
   Butler & Wilson, *194*
   Carnegie, Hattie, *145*
   Caviness, Alice, *144*
   Chanel, *84*
   chessmen, *77*

Jonné, *117*
Lane, Kenneth Jay, *173*
Ledo and Pierre, *139*
malachite, *33*
Mazer Brothers, *137, 178*
paste, *21*
portrait, *22*
post-Depression and war years, 69,
       75, *87–88, 90–91, 100*
   Retro style, 69
Robert Originals, *108*
Schiaparelli, *126–131*
Schreiner, Henry, *120, 124, 179*
Selro, *138*
Sherman, *132*
silver, *26*
Sixties & Seventies, *163, 166, 170,
       173, 175–76, 178–79*
Sorrell, Robert, 207
tortoiseshell, *12*
Trifari, *90–91, 166*
Vendome, *170*
Victorian era, *17–18, 26, 33, 35*
Victorian revival, *141*
Braendle, Gustav, 46
Braque, Georges, 165

Christmas tree, *208*
Coppola e Toppo, *185*
Czech, *43*, 99
D&E, *177*
DeMario, Robert, *118*
DeRosa, *85*
Dior, *109*
dog, *45, 73*
Duettes, 69, *94–95*
elephant, *49, 72, 73, 79, 99*
Eighties & Nineties, *191–94*
Eisenberg, *92–93*
Fahrner, Theodor, 40
fan, *73*
Fifties, *104–105, 109, 112, 114, 116,
       121–25, 127, 133, 136–37, 140,
       143–47, 153*
fish, *49*
flag, *71*
floral, *19, 20, 29, 58, 68, 74, 78,
       80–82, 84–85, 95, 116, 133, 205, 213*
French jet, *30*
frog, *74, 84*
German, *40–41, 49*
hair jewelry, *18–19*
hand, *72*
Har, *136*
Haskell, Miriam, *112, 114*
Hobé, William, *87–88, 147*
horse, *99*
initial, *39, 48*
insects, *15, 30, 45, 59, 92, 99, 105, 191*
Jelly Bellies, *66–67, 72*
Jomaz, *137*
Lane, Kenneth Jay, *164–65, 173*
lion, *165*
lobster, *73*
malachite, *33*
Marion, Helen, *172*
Mazer Brothers, *178*
Mizpah pins, *10–11, 12, 27*
Moini, Iradj, *191*
monkey, *10, 11*

monkey-man, 67
paste, 10–11, 20–21
patriotic, 70–71
phoenix, 133
picture frames, 96
portrait, 18–19, 88
post-Depression and war years,
 64–65, 68, 74–75, 77–85, 87–90,
 92–99
rabbit, 79
Retro style, 64
Sandor, 98
sash pins, 28, 29
Schiaparelli, Elsa, 43, 104, 127
Schreiner, Henry, 105, 121–25
Scottish, 32
seahorses, 95
shoulder, 114
Shulman, Mimi, 193
Silson, 82
Sixties & Seventies, 164–65, 168,
 171–73, 177–78, 185
swivel, 18–19
trembler, 82
Trifari, 89–90, 168
turtle, 49
Twenty-first century, 205, 208, 213
USA, 71
Vendome, 171
Victorian era, 15–16, 18–21, 24,
 27–30, 32–34
Vogue, 65, 83
Vrba, Larry, 208
Bulgari, 207
Bush, Barbara, 163
Butler & Wilson, 194

C
cairngorm, 32, 34–35
Cardin, Pierre, 163
Carnegie, Hattie, 145, 162
Cartier, 41, 52, 68, 79, 90, 134, 135, 207
Castlecliff, 208
Caviness, Alice, 144
celluloid, 41, 61
Celtic Revival style, 46
Chalayan, Hussein, 195

Chanel, Coco, 42, 84, 105, 109, 130,
 193, 198, 206, 207
 jewelry, 84, 102, 110–11, 115,
 155, 188, 190
Clément, Jean, 43
clips, 24, 48, 51, 64
collars, 14, 148–49, 158. See also necklaces
collecting, 212–13
Coppola e Toppo, 107, 160, 165,
 182–85
Coro (Coro Craft/Corocraft), 67, 69,
 72, 94–95, 106–107, 165, 170, 174.
 See also Vendome
Costin, Simon, 195
Courrèges, 163
Crawford, Joan, 65, 104
Cubism, 39, 172
cuffs, 194, 195
cut steel, 10
Czech Republic, 10
 brooches, 43, 99
 figurals, 59
 style, 56

D
D&E, 163, 174, 175–77
Dadaism, 39
Dalí, Salvador, 42
Davis, Bette, 68, 107
de Givenchy, Hubert, 108
DeLillo, 208
DeLizza, William, 165
Delman, 162
DeMario, Robert, 107, 118
demi-parures
 Dior, 151
 Haskell, Miriam, 200–201
 Robert Originals, 119
 Schiaparelli, Elsa, 129
Déon, Michel, 109
Depression, 43, 64
DeRosa, 84, 85, 108–109
de Taxco, Margot, 202
Diana, Lady, 190
Dietrich, Marlene, 65
Dior, 69, 106–107, 109, 120, 151, 162,
 187, 198

Dolce e Gabbana, 195
double-clips, 64
dress clips, 48
DRGM, 50–51
Duettes, 69, 94–95
Dweck, Stephen, 206
Dynasty, 190

E
earrings
 Art Deco and prewar period, 51
 Bakelite, 75
 Carnegie, Hattie, 145
 Chanel, 155
 Coppola e Toppo, 185
 D&E, 174–75, 177
 DeMario, Robert, 118
 de Taxco, Margot, 202
 Dior, 151, 187
 DRGM, 51
 Eighties & Nineties, 194, 200–202
 Elma, 210
 Fifties, 117, 119–20, 124, 127–31,
 136–39, 143, 145–49, 151
 Har, 136
 Haskell, Miriam, 200–201
 Hobé, William, 147
 Jomaz, 137
 Jonné, 117
 Lacroix, Christian, 194
 Ledo and Pierre, 139
 Mazer Brothers, 137
 post-Depression and war years, 75, 90
 Robert Originals, 119
 Schiaparelli, Elsa, 127–31
 Schreiner, Henry, 120, 124, 162
 Selro, 138
 Sixties & Seventies, 162, 170, 174–75,
 177, 185, 187
 Trifari, 90
 Twenty-first century, 210
 Vendome, 170
 Victorian Revival, 143
Easter Egg stones, 165, 177
Egyptian revival, 25, 28, 41

Eighties & Nineties (1980–1999),
 188–203
 bracelets, 190, 195–97, 202
 brooches, 191–94
 cuffs, 194
 demi-parures, 200, 201
 earrings, 194, 200–202
 necklaces, 188, 198–203
 parure, 202
Eisenberg, 41, 66, 68, 92–93, 207
Elizabeth II, Queen, 167
Elma, 210
enamel pins, 67, 69
end-of-day collars, 158
Exposition Internationale des Arts
 Décoratifs et Industriels
 Modernes, 38, 40

F
Fahrner, Theodor, 40, 41, 46
Fashioncraft Jewelry, 119. See also
 Robert Originals
Fifties (1950–1959), 102–159
 bracelets, 106, 108–109, 113, 117,
 120, 124, 126–32, 136–39,
 141–44, 149
 brooches, 104–105, 109, 112, 114,
 116, 121–25, 127, 133, 136–37, 140,
 143–47, 153
 collar sets, 148–49
 demi-parures, 129, 151
 earrings, 117, 119–20, 124, 127–31,
 136–39, 143, 145–49, 151
 necklaces, 102, 110–11, 113–15, 117,
 119–20, 126, 129–31, 134–36, 143,
 145–52, 154–59
 parures, 120, 130–31, 136, 143,
 146–47
figurals
 Art Deco and prewar period, 45, 49
 Bakelite, 45, 88
 bird, 41, 133, 168
 Boucher, Marcel, 68
 butterflies, 59, 168
 Chanel, 84
 Coro, 67
 Czech, 59

dog, *45*
Fifties, *133*
insect, *45, 59, 168*
Jelly Bellies, *66–67, 72*
Lane, Kenneth Jay, *165*
lion, *165*
monkey-man, *67*
post-Depression and war years, *67, 97*
phoenix, *133*
robotic, *97*
Schiaparelli, Elsa, *43*
Sixties & Seventies, *168*
Trifari, *67, 168*
French jet, *14, 23, 30–31. See also* jet
"fruit salad" stones, *91*
fur clips, *24, 48, 51*

G
Galalith, *36*
Garbo, Greta, *65*
Gardner, Ava, *68, 107, 165*
Garne, *174*
Gaultier, Jean Paul, *190, 207*
German jewelry, *40–41, 44, 49, 50–51*
Gernreich, Rudi, *164*
Giacometti, Alberto, *43*
Goossens, *194*
granite, *32–34*
Grès, Madame, *206*
Gripoix, Madame (Maison), *42, 102, 106–107, 115, 198–99*

H
hair jewelry, *12, 18–19*
Halston, *166*
Har, *106, 136*
Hardy, John, *206*
Harlow, Jean, *65*
Harmon, Colette, *211*
Haskell, Miriam, *67, 101, 104, 106–107, 116, 191, 208*
  bracelets, *100, 106, 113*
  brooches, *112, 114*
  demi-parures, *200–201*
  earrings, *200–201*
  necklaces, *62, 101, 113–14, 200–201*

print ad, *66*
prototypes, *100, 107*
Henie, Sonja, *104*
Hepburn, Audrey, *162, 163*
Hess, Frank, *101, 116*
Hobé, William, *68, 86, 87–88, 107, 147*
Hollycraft, *109*

I
Industrial Revolution, *10, 26*

J
Jacquin of Paris, *10*
Jagger, Bianca, *166, 193*
Jean-Pierre, Roger, *106, 107*
Jelly Bellies, *66–67, 72*
jet, *13–14, 22–23, 30–31*
Jomaz, *136, 137*
Jonné, *107, 116, 117*
Joseff of Hollywood, *104*
Juliana, *165, 174*

K
Karan, Donna, *192, 193*
Kawakubo, Rei, *190*
Kempner, Nan, *163*
Kennedy (Onassis), Jacqueline, *162, 165, 190*
KJL. *See* Lane, Kenneth Jay
Klein, Calvin, *167, 193*
Kramer, *107, 174*

L
Lacroix, Christian, *193, 194*
Lagerfeld, Karl, *193*
Lancetti, *165*
Lane, Kenneth Jay, *42, 162–64, 165, 173, 180–81, 190*
Lane, Neil, *206*
Lang, Helmut, *207*
Lanvin, *206–207*
Lauren, Ralph, *206*
Ledo and Pierre, *138, 139*
Leighton, Fred, *206*
Levy, Robert. *See* Robert Originals
lockets, *26, 211*

Lombard, Carole, *104*
love brooches. *See* Mizpah pins
Lucite, *66*
Luckenbooth, *13*

M
Machine Age, *39, 41, 44*
machine cutting, *10*
Macy's, *65*
Maer, Mitchell, *107*
malachite, *13, 33*
marcasite, *10*
Marcel Boucher et Cie. *See* Boucher, Marcel
Margiela, Martin, *195*
Marion, Helen, *165, 172*
Marni, *207*
Mazer Brothers, *68, 79, 134, 136, 137, 178*
Mazer, Joseph, *136*
McQueen, Alexander, *195*
memento mori, *12, 195*
Migeon and Migeon, *194*
Minnelli, Liza, *193*
Miu Miu, *207*
Mizpah pins, *10–11, 12, 27*
Moini, Iradj, *191*
Monet, *65*
Mori, Hanae, *191*
Morris, Robert Lee, *192–93, 206*
Morris, William, *14*
Moss, Eli and Sandy, *67, 107, 114*
motifs
  beetle, *25, 41*
  bows, *65, 93, 98*
  floral, *66, 113*
  of Lacroix, Christian, *193*
  leaf, *38, 126*
  nature, *24, 26, 112–13*
  patriotic jewelry, *66*
  of Pennino Brothers, *65, 80*
  ribbons, *65*
  of Sandor, *98*
  scarab, *25*
  Scottish, *13*
  Victorian era, *11, 13, 24, 25*

mourning jewelry, *12, 195*
Mugler, Thierry, *191*

N
Napier, *65, 104, 207*
necklaces
  Alfandary, Rafael, *167*
  Art Deco and prewar, *36, 38, 40, 45, 47, 50–51, 54–55*
  Bakelite, *38, 45, 50–51, 76*
  Bergamini, Lucy, *203*
  Bonaz, Auguste, *36*
  Boucher, Marcel, *134–35*
  bow, *188*
  Carnegie, Hattie, *145*
  Chanel, *102, 110–11, 115, 155, 188*
  Coppola e Toppo, *160, 182–85*
  Czech enamel, *54–55*
  D&E, *174–75, 177*
  DeRosa, *85*
  de Taxco, Margot, *202*
  Dior, *151, 187*
  DRGM, *50–51*
  Egyptian revival, *25, 28*
  Eighties & Nineties, *188, 198–203*
  Elma, *210*
  Fifties, *102, 110–11, 113–15, 117, 119–20, 126, 129–31, 134–36, 143, 145–52, 154–59*
  floral, *85, 101*
  French jet, *23, 31*
  Gripoix, Maison, *115, 198–99*
  Harmon, Colette, *211*
  Haskell, Miriam, *62, 101, 113–14, 200–201*
  Hobé, William, *86, 147*
  Har, *136*
  insect, *25*
  Jonné, *117*
  Lacroix, Christian, *204*
  Lane, Kenneth Jay, *180–81*
  mesh, *47, 150*
  pâte de verre, *198*
  post-Depression and war years, *62, 76, 85–87, 101*
  Robert Originals, *119*
  Rousselet, Louis, *110–11*
  Schiaparelli, Elsa, *126, 129–31*
  Schreiner, Henry, *120, 159, 179*

Sixties & Seventies, *160, 167, 169–70, 174–75, 177, 179–87*
Sorrell, *209*
Trifari, *169*
Twenty-first century, *204, 209–11*
Vendome, *170*
Victorian era, *16–17, 24, 26, 28, 31*
Norelle, 120

O

Op Art, 164

P

parures. See also demi-parures
  Carnegie, Hattie, *145*
  Coppola e Toppo, *185*
  D&E, *175, 177*
  de Taxco, Margot, *202*
  Eighties & Nineties, *202*
  Fifties, *120, 130–31, 136, 143, 146–47*
  Har, *136*
  Hobé, William, *147*
  Schiaparelli, Elsa, *130–31*
  Schreiner, Henry, *120*
  Sixties & Seventies, *170, 175, 177, 185*
  Vendome, *170*
pâte de verre, *198*
Patou, Jean, 38
patriotic jewelry, 61, 65–66, 69–71
pearls, 40, 106, 107
pendants, *16, 25, 26, 167*
Pennino Brothers, 64–65, *80–81*
Peretti, Elsa, 167
Petronzio, Millie, 101
Pforzheim, Germany, 41, 46
Philippe, Alfred, 66, 72, 90, *91*
pins. See also brooches
  Duettes, 69, *94–95*
  Eisenberg, 68
  enamel, 67, 69
  Mizpah, 10–11, *12, 27*
  sash, *28–29*
  tremblant, 69
  Trifari, 67
plaid jewelry, *34–35*
plique-à-jour, *15*
Poiret, Paul, 38, 42
Polcini, Ralph, 138
portrait jewelry, *12, 18–19, 22,* 88

post-Depression and war years (1935–1949), 62–101
  attitudes, 65
  Bakelite, 66, 73, 74, 75
  bracelets, 69, 75, *87–88, 90–91, 100*
  brooches, *64–65, 68, 74–75, 77–79, 80–85, 87–90, 92–99*
  Duettes, *94, 95*
  earrings, 75, 90
  figurals, *66–67, 84, 97*
  Jelly Bellies, *66–67, 72*
  necklaces, 62, 76, *85–87, 101*
  patriotic jewelry, 65–66, *69–71*
Prada, Miuccia, 206
prewar period. See Art Deco and prewar period
prototype jewelry, *100,* 107
Pucci, 165

Q

Quant, Mary, 162
Queen Elizabeth II, 167
Queen Victoria, 10, *11, 12,* 13, 14

R

Rabanne, Paco, 107, 163
Rafael, *166, 167*
Renaissance Revival style, *56*
Retro-style jewelry, *64,* 69
rings, 11, 64
Robert Originals, *108, 119*
Rousselet, Louis, *110–11*
Ruskin, John, 14

S

Saint Laurent, Yves, 194, 207
Sandor, 69, *98*
Sandoz, Gérard, 40
Sant'Angelo, Giorgio di, 163
sash pins, *28–29*
Scemama, Roger, 107
Schiaparelli, Elsa, 42, 43, *108–109,* 130, *193,* 207
  bracelets, *126–31*
  brooches, 43, *104, 127*
  demi-parure, *129*
  earrings, *127–31*
  figurals, 43
  motifs, *126*
  necklaces, *126, 129–31*
  parures, *130–31*
  print ad, *107*

Schlumberger, Jean, 43
Schon, 165
Schrager, *117*
Schreiner, Henry, *105,* 107, 120, *121–25, 159, 162,* 165, *179*
Scottish jewelry, 13, *32–35*
Selro, 138
serpents, 11
Shearer, Norma, 65
shells, 66, 67
Sherman, Gustave, 108, 132
Shulman, Mimi, *193*
Silson, 69, 82
Sixties & Seventies (1960–1979), 160–187
  bracelets, *163, 166, 170, 173, 175–76, 178–79*
  brooches, *164–65, 168, 171–73, 177–78, 185*
  earrings, *162, 170, 174–75, 177, 185, 187*
  necklaces, 160, 167, *169–70, 174–75, 177, 179–87*
  parures, *170, 175, 177, 185*
  pendants, 167
Sorrell, Robert, *191–92,* 207, *209*
Spencer, Lady Diana, 190
Stras, Georges, 10
Surrealism, 39, 43, 130
Swarovski, 40, 106, 207

T

Taylor, Elizabeth, 163, 165
Tiffany, 167
Trifari, 41, 65–67, 72, 88, 90, 104, 106, 164, 207
  jewelry, *67, 89–91, 166, 168–69*
Trigère, 120
Turner, Lana, 104
Tutankhamen, 41, 42
Twenty-first century (2000–present), 204–213
  bracelet, *207*
  brooches, *205, 208, 213*
  earrings, *210*
  necklaces, *204, 209, 210, 211*
Twiggy, 162

U

Ungaro, Emmanuel, 163

V

Valentino, 165, 206, 207
Van Cleef & Arpels, 41, 52, 90, *135*
Vendome, 69, 165, *170–71*
Versace, Gianni, 194
Victoria, Queen, 10, *11,* 12, 13, 14
Victorian era and Art Nouveau (1837–1910), 8–35
  bracelets, *17, 18, 26, 33,* 35
  brooches, *15–16, 18–21, 24, 27–30, 32–34*
  hair jewelry, 12, *18–19*
  jet, *13–14*
  memento mori, 12
  motifs, 11, *13, 24, 25*
  necklaces, *16–17, 24, 26, 28, 31*
  Scottish jewelry, 13, *32–35*
Victorian Revival jewelry, *141, 143*
Vionnet, Madame, 38
Vogue (magazine), 64, 105
Vogue (manufacturer), 65, 69, 82, *83*
von Furstenberg, Diane, 166, 191
Vrba, Larry, 101, 191, *208*
Vreeland, Diana, 104, 195

W

Warhol, Andy, 193
Weiss and Coventry, 174
Westwood, Vivienne, 167, 190
Whitby, England, 13, 14, 22
Winter, Frances, 106
wood, 62, 66, 67

Y

Yamamoto, Yohji, 195
Yurman, David, 206

Editorial Director
WANDA NOWAKOWSKA

Project Editor
ALISON MACLEAN

Book Design
COSTA LECLERC DESIGN INC.

Text
RITA SILVAN

Photo Research
BAO-NGHI NHAN

Production Manager
SANDRA L. HALL

Publisher
OLIVER SALZMANN

Vice President, Business Affairs and Production
SUSAN BARRABLE

Printed by
LOTUS PRINTING, CHINA

FABULOUS
FAKES

was produced by
Madison Press Books